CUT 'N' RUN

CUT 'N' RUN

Frank Deford

The Viking Press / New York

First published in 1973 by The Viking Press, Inc.
625 Madison Avenue, New York, N.Y. 10022

Published simultaneously in Canada by
The Macmillan Company of Canada Limited

SBN 670-25184-4

Library of Congress catalog card number: 72-79003
Printed in U.S.A. by The Book Press Inc.

Carol, this is for you, Baby Cakes

Contents

CUT 'N' RUN

1

The Ensuing Kickoff

Jerry and Rosalie Start's was the first pro football generation. Pro football was as crucial to their lives as religion or the harvest or depression had been to American generations past. The Starts (she was Rosalie Gail Totter of Bonnie View Drive, Towson 4, Maryland, before her marriage) fell between two stools: nuclear war and social revolution. Their generation had pro football. It wasn't much, but it was all they had as a signature.

As the Starts and their contemporaries grew up in the 1950s, football not only replaced baseball as the national sport but, more important, became a true cause of social change. Pro football could draw huge metropolitan populations together while simultaneously driving families apart. Beforehand, only selected wars had been capable of that.

Many people came to say, in fact, that pro football bore a close relationship to war, but Rosalie would have none of that. To her, pro football seemed just like sex, particularly all the leading up and looking forward—a new liaison and a new climax week after week. Baseball was an old dependable, like marriage; it was a regular sort of everyday thing. Football was a good lay, to plot, to savor, and then to lie about in a barbershop somewhere.

Rosalie was no extremist in her views, either, for the Starts were only a run-of-the-mill pro football household. Rosalie seldom nursed any grudges toward Jerry past April, and once they even had sex together on a week night in November. As fans went, Jerry was quite well behaved. He still drank a lot of National Bohemian beer during the games and wore a faded old high-school maroon football jersey, Number 83, but it had been years since he had broken anything valuable, such as the TV set, while watching a game. He still cared for his two children in season, remembered to have the snow tires put on, and went to the office regularly. Jerry even kept on giving to the church of his choice, although he was unable to worship from Trinity through Epiphany inasmuch as church services were always scheduled on game days; apparently, the rector didn't have season tickets.

That Jerry was only an ordinary pro football fan was of small consolation to Rosalie, however. It still seemed to her that for any wife the pro football season was like having four additional menstruations each month. Besides, relatively normal as Jerry appeared, there was no telling what effect his devotion to pro ball might have on the children. At this time, late in 1967, Jerry Jr. was four, and Kimberly almost two. Rosalie, a recent initiate in the local LaLeche League, feared that as the twig was bent, so the tree inclined.

And what could she tell them of their father when he bellowed strange noises of joy and anguish from the club cellar and then bolted upstairs for another beer, gurgling and disarrayed? Rosalie tried to keep the children far from him at such times.

This particular Sunday night, as the Colts played the Rams On-The Coast, she had herded them into the family room, where they could watch a program about antelopes on the little old black-and-white set. Naturally Jerry commandeered the color set for football. Rosalie laid out their dinner of mashed potatoes and grape Kool-Aid, mixed a frozen banana daiquiri for herself, picked out *This Week* magazine from the Sunday paper, and began reading the cover story on how the trampoline boom was a threat to a healthy America.

Suddenly Jerry was upon them, reaching for another beer and taking the opportunity to bring them up to date. He was ecstatic. "Clutcheroony," he cried. "Checking off to catch the blitz, old Johnny U clicks with Orr on a post pattern for pay dirt. How 'bout that, Baby Cakes? Would you believe an upset?"

"Would you believe you look like a shipwreck?" Rosalie replied. In fright, Halfback, the family schnauzer, scampered under a chair. Jerry suddenly turned and rushed back downstairs. "Back to live action," he cried. "My God, it's almost the ensuing kickoff."

"You can come out now, Halfback," Rosalie said softly. "The White Tornado has gone again."

"Why does Daddy act like that sometimes?" little Jerry asked.

"Hush, child," Rosalie said, tousling his hair. "It's only The Football. When the moon that comes after Christmas is full, the evil spirits will depart from him, and he will be your father again."

"Mommy, Mommy, what's that mean?"

"It means the damn season is almost over," Rosalie explained, and she bade the children sit round her feet and listen. "Once, when I was a child, growing up long ago, the season would end at Thanksgiving. Then Christmas; now January. By the time Kimberly is grown, it will last fifty weeks a year. They'll set aside two weeks late in March for a mating season. Like those antelopes on the TV. Do you want some more grape Kool-Aid? It's very good. I made it myself from an old family recipe."

Little Jerry handed up his cup and, seeing this, Kimberly stumbled up and put her cup out too. Rosalie filled them both. "Hey," little Jerry exclaimed, "she didn't eat all her mashed potatoes."

"The poor thing is destined to grow up into an antelope's life," Rosalie said. "Let's let her have some grape Kool-Aid. It's the least we can do."

The fact is, Rosalie really did view the Colts as straight one-on-one competition for her man, and Rosalie, who was some honey, was not used to being beaten in any competition where a man was the issue. Rosalie took after her father, whose side had all the looks. She was tall and leggy and dark like him, and she had also inherited his deep eyes and dimples. Luckily, from her mother Rosalie had gotten the very best thing her mother had, which was her boobs. Rosalie's were just loaded with charisma. Also from her mother, she got freckles. Very few dark-complexioned people have freckles, but Rosalie did, and it was a fantastic arrangement, especially when she had a good tan. It made men wild for her, as if she were some hot-blooded mulatto.

Rosalie had fallen back naturally on all these assets when first she sensed that she was losing Jerry to The Football. None of the usual sure-fire workaday little gimmicks succeeded, however. Jerry just kept watching the games and fondling his regulation NFL football that had been autographed by two live Colts ("Best wishes, Ordelle Braase" and "Yours, 43, Lenny Lyles"). Finally, in exasperation, Rosalie came downstairs late one Sunday afternoon, stood right next to the TV set, systematically removed all her clothes, spread her feet some distance apart, put her hands on her hips, and pouted, the way she had seen girls stand on dirty-magazine covers.

Possibly in a lopsided AFL game it might have worked, but Rosalie happened to pick a wild series of downs in a tough MUST-game with the Lions, and she didn't stand a chance. Jerry was not at all aroused, nor even amused. He just growled, "Watch you don't knock against the horizontal," and then he said, "Judas Priest, why does Unitas keep trying the end runs," and, "Moore is open on the down-and-out every time," and things of that nature. Rosalie finally began to get a chill, so, with resignation, she hung her bra and panties on each ear of the antenna and her stockings on the channel selector, trudged up the stairs, and took a hot shower.

This happened when the Starts had just moved into a row house in Far Lake Estates, and three neighbor children, Carl and Davey Bailey, eight and six respectively, and Tim Wyatt, five and a half, saw Rosalie in the buff as she proceeded up the stairs past the window that didn't have the curtains up yet. They told their parents. Gwen Bailey called Rosalie right up to admonish her, and Herb Wyatt came out next door and began raking leaves even though dusk was falling.

Certainly, in those early days of marriage, Rosalie could not imagine that things were only going to get worse. She was no novice to football, either. In high school Rosalie went steady for almost two years with none other than Toby Geyser, who is still recognized as the greatest player ever to come out of the state of Maryland. But Rosalie found that the professional football fan was an entirely different beast from any mere player. The fan was engulfed by the thing.

There were those glad to profit by this craving, too. For instance, in the early 1960s, when Rosalie and Jerry were first married, only the Colts were on television in Baltimore on Sundays, and then only for the road games. This was known as The Policy. Soon, however, The Policy was modified so that other league games, from other time zones, were also piped into

Baltimore. This made television double-headers. Also, there were suddenly whole other double-headers coming from the new American Football League, which was invented by another channel. Although Jerry professed to despise this interloper league, never passing up an opportunity to characterize the AFL as "the Mickey Mouse league," this bias never interfered with his devoted attendance before the set when any nonconflicting AFL game was offered, even those that involved Denver, with its funny striped stockings.

As the years passed, Rosalie did garner some consolation from the knowledge that their happy home was not alone in suffering from this dread social disease. For a long time she was reluctant to admit to friends how different Jerry was during the season, but once, at a girls' duckpin bowling party at Johnny Unitas's Colt Lanes, she introduced the subject and was amazed at how many of her friends immediately followed her lead and began to spill their very guts out too. Nearly to a housewife, they all had the same sad accounts to tell. Rosalie then decided that this madness must be endemic only to Baltimore men, and she came to despise her home town. She even grew chary of soft-shell crabs. Historically, anyway, Rosalie was on firm ground. The passion for professional football that swept over the whole land in the sixties had had its genesis in Baltimore in the early fifties, when the town was awarded the Colts franchise in the NFL. Baltimore, a large but undistinguished city, generally ignored and mispronounced Ball-*tee*-more by outsiders— or, that failing, vilified by them—found in its champion "big-league" pro team something special for itself, a lance to tilt against the more fashionable metropolises that looked down their noses at it.

So by the 1960s, if pro football was a plague over all the republic, it had first been infected by Baltimore. Rosalie did not fully appreciate that the whole nation had become unbalanced until she and Jerry went on a special excursion to New York to see the Colts play the Giants at Yankee Stadium. The trip included reserved-seat tickets on the Pennsylvania Railroad in private cars, domicile at the Roosevelt Hotel, guaranteed tickets to a fading Broadway musical, and discount prices (including a complimentary cocktail) at any of several midtown restaurants.

Rosalie agreed to the trip because it was a chance to see New York and to visit with her old college roommate from Sweet Briar, Mary Beth Trainor. She was now married to Tom Potter, a fast-rising account executive who was personally on speaking terms with several network newscasters. Rosalie was startled to learn from Mary Beth that Tom and his friends were the same way about the New York Giants as Jerry and the men in Baltimore were about the Colts. Rosalie was really impressed. If Mary Beth and Tom had lived in Philadelphia, say, or Cleveland, this news would have meant nothing to Rosalie. But New York was something else altogether, for she had grown up instructed in the faith that to do, wear, or think anything (except those things dealing with Jews and colored people) was okay so long as it prevailed in New York. This made Jerry a more fashionable kind of lunatic.

For that matter, from what Mary Beth let on about Tom, Jerry seemed almost a mild case, "pro-football-wise," as Mary Beth explained it. Tom Potter bet heavily on games, drank hard liquor in large amounts while they were in progress, and sometimes would even go with rowdy friends all the way to a motel near Hartford, Connecticut, to see the Giants on television. By contrast, at least Jerry maintained a physical presence. Many of the neighbors were none the wiser that he was totally transformed during the season.

Of course, the reason that Jerry retained some composure was that he required himself to keep complicated charts during all the games that did not involve the Colts. Jerry was a stock-

broker, and he was convinced that there was a correlation between the number of first downs, punts, and fumble-recoveries
that a team made and how the stocks of the companies in that
team's city would fare in the following week. That is, for instance, if the Detroit Lions charted the right number of first
downs, punts, and fumble-recoveries, it was time to get into
Chrysler.

After years of cross-checking his theories, Jerry decided to test
them for real one week, and the results were truly incredible.
Every stock he bought soared at least 18 points that week. Of
course, that was also the week the Dow-Jones averages climbed
64 points and the American Stock Exchange index—the whole
index—split two for one, and 463 out of 472 listings on the over-
the-counter went up. As a consequence, Jerry confided to
Rosalie that he did not think it altogether fair to claim that his
theories had been completely borne out.

Nonetheless, she was grateful enough for the time that it took
him to offer her these revelations. In season any ordinary fan,
such as Jerry, was required to perform his devotions every day
of the week, not just Sunday. The foreplay of pro football is
considerably more involved and lengthy—if not also more vital
—than the game itself. There was seldom any free time left
over to enjoy shared experiences with Rosalie.

Sundays, Jerry was either at Memorial Stadium if the Colts
were at home, or he was rooted downstairs to the television if
they were away. Mondays he gave up much of his day at the
office and all of his concentration to attend the regular weekly
luncheon meeting of the Colt Stampede fan club. Once, in a
drawing at the Stampede, Jerry won the door prize—a regulation
Colt helmet. He kept this on a shelf downstairs in the club
cellar along with other precious Colt artifacts, and a picture of
Rosalie and the kids as well.

Tuesdays, Jerry never came home until the wee hours of the

next morning. First he was required to attend his weekly National Guard meeting. Then afterward he always went out with some of the other Guardsmen to play APBA football, a scientific board game, and the players in Jerry's APBA league had draft meetings and trades and pre-season games and a regular season. Wednesday nights Jerry was so tired from staying up late the night before to play APBA that he was forced to take it easy, isolating himself so that he could examine pro football journals and watch NFL highlights from the past Sunday's game on TV. Thursday evening was Colt highlights on television. By Fridays, although there was no electronic exercise, Jerry was in such a stew over the approaching game Sunday that he often drank to excess and was generally incoherent even if he did not. Saturdays he was hung over, and although his buddy Reds Ritchie usually came over to speculate on Colt strategy, Jerry would always go to bed early, oblivious to Rosalie, whether she chanced to be lying beside him or not, because "I need my sleep—it's going to be a big day come tomorrow."

On those few occasions when Rosalie still bothered to offer a token complaint about this weekly schedule, Jerry would get huffy and reply, "It's just a game, for Chrissake. Would you like it better if I were out chasing women?" This particular Sunday night, as the kids became engrossed with the antelopes and Jerry remained downstairs with the Colts, Rosalie began musing more seriously on his response. She put *This Week* aside and, sipping her banana daiquiri, she decided that she might indeed prefer the alternative since it was her understanding that married men who chased after other women did it more on their own time, and also they brought home flowers and jewels to their wives and took their children to zoos and amusement parks because of their guilty consciences.

Rosalie was shaken from this consideration only by the telephone, which she rushed to answer because she knew, of course, that it was long-distance. Obviously, no one in Baltimore would be calling anyone else in the last minutes of a Colt game. Still, she could not possibly have been prepared for who it was and was still in some shock when Jerry came upstairs a bit later. Of course, in his happy estate, he took no notice of her.

"Daddy's crying," Jerry Jr. told Kimberly, and Jerry took that cue to explain how grown-ups could cry with happiness. Employing salt- and pepper-shakers as key personnel, with Kimberly's leftover mashed potatoes serving as the line of scrimmage, he outlined some of the bigger plays that had brought victory for the Colts. Kimberly crawled up on his lap. She knew her father now, the strong man who could fix anything around the house and play honky-tonk songs on the piano. He was himself again. The long, hard day before the TV set was through. There were no more games from any more time zones, from anywhere. There was nothing left for him now but to wait until the eleven-o'clock news to hear the reconfirmation of all the scores that he had just heard on the post-game wrap-up.

"God, what an incredible day," he said, putting an arm around Rosalie's shoulder as if she were the teammate who had just made a tough block. He tended to this sort of comrade's affection in season. Every now and then Jerry would even forget himself altogether and slap Rosalie on the rear instead of kissing her.

He steered her into the living room and collapsed on the sofa. Normally Rosalie would not let him sit there in his beer-stained, sweaty football-watching clothes, but it had been Scotch-Garded only recently, and besides, since the phone call, she didn't much care anyway. Jerry was a tall man, with boyish looks and even a handsome figure if he could remember to keep his weak chin sticking out and never to wear Bermuda shorts. Now, though, sprawled out on the sofa, he seemed curiously old and attenuated.

"It only proves once again," Jerry expostulated, "that on any given day, any team in pro football can beat any other. There was no tomorrow for the Colts if they lost this one. What heart." Jerry pounded his own with his beer can for emphasis. "Do you know what this win means? Do you know?"

Rosalie admitted that she did not.

"It means that instead of being out of the whole 1967 title picture, the Colts now have a chance to clinch first place in the Coastal Division next week. If we beat the Packers next week, we win the division, no matter what Los Angeles does."

"No matter what Los Angeles does?" Rosalie asked dutifully.

"No matter what," Jerry assured her. "If we can just beat the Packers here next Saturday. Would you believe this town will be buzzing all week?"

"Uh-huh."

"Would you believe pandemonium?"

Rosalie, whose mind was still far away, forgot to say "Uh-huh" this time.

"Would you believe pandemonium all week?" Jerry persisted.

Rosalie said, "Uh-huh," so Jerry stood up and clapped her on the shoulder. "Don't you just know it, Baby Cakes," he said, and he started marching back and forth, intermittently humming the Colts' fight song and inserting the lyrics where he knew them. Actually, though he had heard that song hundreds of times, all he really knew was the part that went ". . . and put the ball across the line," so mostly he just thundered the refrain: "Fight, fight, fight!"

"By the way," Rosalie said during a hum segment, "Toby Geyser called. He's coming to town to play for the Colts next week."

Jerry stopped short, as if the whole Colt band had been run over by a train. Smirking, and much resembling a majorette, Rosalie strode past him and out of the room.

2

Check-Off

Only a few hours before, Major Toby Geyser, 0-98407, had been relaxing in his room in the BQ at Fort Belvoir, Virginia, waiting for the telecast of the Redskins-Cowboys game to begin. He had borrowed a portable TV and was looking forward to a few peaceful hours by himself for the first time in days. Everyone had been placing demands on him, because on Thursday, President Johnson himself had pinned the Congressional Medal of Honor upon Toby's chest in special ceremonies held in the Rose Garden of the White House.

But now, just as the Cowboys starters were being introduced, there was an urgent knock on Toby's door. Grudgingly he pulled himself up out of his chair and opened the door. A full colonel was standing there. "Major Geyser," he said, "I have special orders for you." And he displayed them like an eviction notice. Toby threw his uniform on immediately and followed the officer out to an Army car, where another bird colonel was serving as driver. The automobile proceeded directly to the

Pentagon, and the two colonels escorted Toby inside at the River Entrance.

They steered him along the E Ring, then cut down a corridor to an unmarked staircase. They wound down at least three floors, to well below ground level, then went out a heavy door, through a labyrinth of hallways, to a door marked: NO ENTRANCE, AUTHORIZED MILITARY PERSONNEL ONLY, SA-264.

One colonel took out a blue key and inserted it in the lock. He switched it a half-turn and then withdrew his key. Then the other colonel pulled out a beige key, inserted it, and completed the full turn. The door flew open, and the three men stepped into a small chamber. The door closed automatically behind them, and they were almost immediately blinded by flashbulb explosions. "Christ, I wish they'd hurry up with all this top-secret bullshit," one of the colonels said. "At this rate, we're going to miss the whole first half."

"You'd think it would be just as easy to save the country on a Monday afternoon," the other replied, just as the door opened and Toby saw a huge war room dominated by a large electric map of the United States looming over a massive oval table and numerous high leather chairs. There were only three men present, and they all moved forward to salute the newcomers. Toby's two escort colonels returned the salute, did an about face, and moved back into the compartment.

"Major Geyser," said the compact little officer who approached him, "this is indeed my pleasure. I'm Major General Adam Admire." And, disdaining the formal salute, he reached out and shook Toby's hand. "General Carlton Samuels, Colonel Roger Beardsley," he went on, completing the introductions. They showed Toby to the table and bade him take a seat. He recognized General Samuels, but it was General Admire, a trim man who had given up eyebrows, who began the briefing. He did not mince words.

"Major Geyser," he began, "you have been brought to the secret headquarters of DANG. That's D-A-N-G. That stands for Defense Against National Guard, and it is perhaps the most secret aspect of the entire US Armed Forces, bar none. DANG is dedicated to the possibility that someday the National Guard may rise up and try to take over the United States."

"The National Guard?" Toby said.

"Granted, it's a remote possibility," General Admire went on, "but the chance does exist, and, as a consequence, DANG was established several years ago to save this country in that unlikely event. Should an attempted National Guard *coup* occur I would automatically be issued special orders that would place under my command every regular in the US Armed Forces."

"Yes sir," Toby said in some awe.

"DANG is, as you can imagine, a vital defense mechanism," General Admire went on, chewing some licorice. "Nevertheless, if the word ever got out that the federal government here in Washington, D.C., had established a force calculated to squash the National Guard, there would be hell to pay with your governors and what-all in the states. Obviously the utmost secrecy is imperative. Savvy?"

"Oh, yes sir."

"In fact, now that you are aware of the operation, there is a total of only seventeen persons, military and civilian, in the entire US of A who are aware of the existence of DANG. I needn't tell you, Major, that you have undergone the most extensive security clearances." Toby nodded again, and he mentioned in passing that he had never even imagined that such a thing as DANG existed.

"That's how the US stays one jump ahead of the other fellow," General Samuels interjected.

"Of course, I don't want you to think, Major," General Admire added quickly, "that we are in danger of jumping the gun with our weekend warriors. Savvy? In fact, I want to assure you that complete command of the Army will not pass to me until we have exhausted a preliminary period known as Phase One."

"What is Phase One?" Toby inquired.

"Phase One takes advantage of computer calculations which show that any special exertion on the part of the National Guard will result in its destroying itself without the need of any outside agency."

"You mean—"

"Yes, to be brutal, Major, the National Guard is so totally incompetent that no matter how many times we have conducted hypothetical computer assaults, the Guard always ends up shooting and killing itself. Except every now and then it gets lucky."

"Then what?" Toby asked.

"Then it merely gets captured," General Admire explained.

"Oh."

"Ahh, but hang on. These are all computer exercises, and computers are run by civilians, and they are not perfect, so we can never altogether dismiss the possibility that somehow the Guard will survive and we will be required to move on to Phase Two. You're familiar with French, Major?"

"Yes sir, a little."

"Good, because Phase Two is the real *raison d'être* for DANG. In Phase Two we become the force that protects our American citizens—all of them, regardless of race, color, or creed—from the National Guard."

"Yes sir, I understand," Toby said.

General Admire rose and began to pace purposefully. "Good. Affirmative," he said. "Possessing this information is a vital trust and not necessarily related to your primary mission."

"But I don't know what my primary mission is, sir," Toby

said. "I thought I was temporarily assigned to Fort Belvoir. I thought I was just supposed to help coach and play on the post football team for a while. Until I was reassigned."

"Well, effective this morning, you're reassigned. Savvy?" General Admire winked. "Colonel Beardsley, will you resume the briefing?"

Beardsley got up and opened his briefcase. From it he withdrew a sheaf of newspaper clippings, and he threw them onto the table in front of Toby. Toby recognized some of them—the Washington *Post* and *Star*, the New York *Times*, the Los Angeles *Times*, his home-town Baltimore *Sun*. All of them were similar in that they featured the Associated Press Wirephoto of Toby receiving the Medal of Honor from the President. He then noticed that the other papers came from every section of the country. Many of them also used an old picture that showed Toby scoring the winning touchdown in the Army-Navy game his senior year. His afternoon home-town paper, the Baltimore *News-Post*, took up virtually the whole front page with even more pictures. One showed him as all-state halfback at Towson High in 1958. Another showed him when he was a Rhodes Scholar, at Oxford, being introduced to the Queen after he had almost single-handedly whipped Cambridge in Rugby for the third year running. Another showed him with Miss World in Vietnam, after she threatened to leave the Bob Hope Christmas Show and stay with him at the front. A final photograph showed Toby after the Rose Garden ceremony, conversing with Maryland Governor Spiro T. Agnew. He had been invited to attend after the President's staff ascertained that the Governor was still in favor of the war; also, both he and Toby came from Towson.

"Well?" Colonel Beardsley asked.

"Got a lot of coverage in the papers, didn't it?" Toby replied. All the brass smiled at his humble naïveté. "That's not the half of it, Major." Beardsley chuckled. "You not only made every front page in the country, you're making every magazine. You made Huntley-Brinkley, Walter Cronkite. You even made some weather forecasts and traffic helicopters. Johnny Carson wants you. And let me tell you: they all love your ass."

Toby blushed. "Tell him about the fucking hillbilly," General Samuels said.

"Yeah," Beardsley said, "we got a telegram yesterday from some country-and-western singer that he's recording a new song called 'The Ballad of War Zone C,' all about how you won the medal."

"How do you like them apples?" General Samuels cried. He was coming to life, and now he grabbed Toby affectionately by a shoulder blade and mumbled a few friendly obscene phrases. A bear of a man, a Congressional Medal of Honor winner himself, and an inspirational leader of the Inchon Landing, Samuels had been immortalized in Korea by a comment a GI made to a newspaper reporter after Samuels had personally led an assault up Hill 459. According to the journalist, the dogface had spotted Samuels at the very point of the assault force, as he raised a hand and cried, "I fight for one Uncle Sam and I fight with another." Thereafter, General Samuels had not been known to discourage the use of "Unc" as a familiar form of address. What a surprise, Toby thought, to find that old Unc Sam was associating in the command of DANG.

Now Samuels rolled back in his chair and thought for effect. "How long have you been back in the States, Major?"

"Well, let's see. I got back the end of October. About a month."

Samuels nodded. "Well, then, you've been back long enough to know we've got something of a little problem here with the bleeding-heart liberals, the Commie dupes, and what have you."

General Admire came in. "It's hard to believe, Major, it's

hard to believe, but there are some Americans who want to back off Vietnam, abandon our obligations, desert our Asian friends, walk away from our treaty commitments. It's hard to believe."

"It's hard to believe," Toby said. "Boy, yes sir, I know."

"No," General Admire said. "It's not so hard to believe when you see American citizens marching on their own Pentagon, disagreeing with our President. It's not so hard to believe anything."

"Yes sir," Toby said.

"There was even some nut priest up in Baltimore the other day pouring blood on draft records," Unc Sam noted.

"That's my home town," Toby said.

"A home-town priest pouring blood on draft records," General Admire said, shaking his head. "It's hard to believe."

"It sure is," Toby said.

"No," said General Admire. "It's not so hard to believe when you got a bunch of them trying to get Bobby Kennedy to go up against the President—and now this week this McCarthy actually into it. Then you can believe anything."

"You sure can," said Toby.

"Right," cried Admire. "I'm glad you understand that all this dissension is coming at just the wrong time. You know that if we can get just another two-three hundred thousand trained people over to Nam to fix their little red wagon, we'll have the whole shootin' match over by spring. Savvy?"

"Oh, yes sir, I know."

"The other thing is, the thing that particularly involves us, is that there is some talk starting up again about activating the National Guard and sending that over there."

"Holy shit, we just can't have that," Beardsley cried.

"We're having enough trouble fighting those dinks without having to contend with the Guard too," Unc added. "The way the Guard operates, like a bunch of monkeys fucking foot-balls, we might be bogged down in Nam for another four-five years."

"Of course, Unc is exaggerating, Major." Admire chuckled. "But we must avoid any situation where the National Guard might be called up. One way is to do everything we can to get the country a hundred per cent back on the right track behind the Army." He turned, dropped a finger at Beardsley, and sat down. The colonel rose and looked down at Toby.

"This is where you start to come in, Major Geyser," he said at last. "These clippings that you got were the most fantastic publicity that the military has received in months. Even the Blue Angels can't touch you. It astounded everyone, and I do mean everyone—let's just say that you were cleared for this mission on the highest authority."

"Savvy?" Admire whispered.

"Major," Beardsley declared, "the whole United States Army is prepared to hitch its wagon to your star."

Unc Sam jumped up, threw his seat back and his arms out with such force that Toby thought he might sing, pray, or tap dance. Instead, he just bellowed. "You stand for the old-fashioned, red-blooded, true-blue American values. You're a commissioned officer, All-American, a Heisman Trophy winner, Rhodes Scholar, a Congressional Medal of Honor winner. You're good-looking, you're neat, you're smart, you're strong, and you got a haircut. You don't look like a piece of pussy, like everybody else is starting to."

Beardsley reached back into his briefcase and pulled out a copy of orders. Skimming, he read from them: "Effective 0900 27 November 1967—that's tomorrow, Monday morning—you, Major Geyser, are to depart Belvoir and report on TDy. as an adviser with the National Guard in Baltimore. You are allowed to take civilian housing. Coincidental with this assignment, you

will join the Baltimore Colts professional football team and play
with them for the balance of the regular league season—"

"Wait a minute," Toby said, "I haven't even talked to the
Colts in five years now, since they took me in the NFL draft."

Admire placed a fatherly hand on Toby's forearm. "That's
being taken care of, Toby. You've been working out for almost
a month with the Belvoir post team, haven't you?"

"Yes sir."

"Working *over* the opposition is more like it," Unc Sam bellowed. "I heard you got six touchdowns just the other day
against Andrews Air Force Base."

"Five, sir," said Toby.

"Well, good enough," said Admire. "You're back in All-
American form. And in the NFL all you got to face is civilians.
Savvy? Even if you get in for just a few plays, your value to the
Colts and pro football is immeasurable. I don't have to tell you,
Major, that you are the greatest college player of the decade,
maybe of the whole modern era. People have been waiting for
years now just to see old 22 back out there on the gridiron
again."

"We're in the process of producing a half-hour film of your
most spectacular college plays," Beardsley said. "The sponsor is
Army Recruiting. We figure that by Friday or Saturday we can
clear time for it on at least a hundred, maybe two hundred TV
stations around the country."

"The FCC will be real interested at license-renewal time
about what stations didn't want that show," Unc Sam said.

"We are prepared to show CBS figures that your debut on
national television next Saturday will increase their ratings by
as much as three million homes," Admire added. "If the Colts
or the NFL need a little pressure to come around, I can assure
you that the network will be on their fannies. Savvy?"

"I got here on short notice," Unc Sam cried, waving some

papers, "the signatures of seventeen senators and sixty-two congressmen from states without pro football franchises, urging an immediate reopening of the antitrust charges against pro football. Of course, now, these legislators have also indicated a willingness to forget this little matter if a certain returning war hero is permitted a chance to play. The nation needs you, Major. You are the best thing we got since Sergeant York and that half-assed turkey gobble of his."

Toby sat upright and tried to smile modestly. "You see, with you we can really drive a point home," Admire said. "Are you familiar with British history, Major? You see, it's like Wellington explained this one time how they really loosened up for this particular battle on the sandlots. Well, we can make the same point about football and beating the Communists. Savvy?"

"It's a fine how-do-you-do," Samuels said, "that the only thing this country will support any more is football. Not wars, not democracy, just football."

Beardsley glanced at his watch. "Major, have you any questions to ask us?"

"Well, yes sir. You know, what exactly is required of me?"

"Your primary obligation is to yourself as a football player," Beardsley replied. "You're not that valuable to us if you're screwing up on the field. But off the field, just by your demeanor, your military bearing—that's where you can really score points for us."

"We're trying to get you as many speaking engagements as possible," Unc Sam said. "High schools and boys' clubs and orphans and crippled children and general inspirational crap like that."

"We just want you to get the US people solidly behind Vietnam—and we want you to tell everybody how important the National Guard is here on the home front," Admire explained. "Savvy?"

Toby nodded. The general cleared his throat and took another piece of licorice. "Major," he finally said, "I'm sure we all want to get out of here and go home and watch the Redskins' game on the tube, but first there is one other vital item. Yours is, really, a dual mission. Are you familiar with architecture?" Toby said he was, somewhat. "Well, good, because this is sort of a split-level assignment. All right, Beardsley, you pick it up."

The colonel assumed his briefing voice again. "Yes, Major, I think you can understand that if it were just a matter of your playing football for the Colts this entire assignment could have been handled by the public-information officers here at a low echelon. But when we discovered that your football draft rights were held by the Colts, we decided that there was an opportunity to employ you on another front. In this regard, you should be advised that this headquarters actually houses *two* secret military arms. DANG, under General Admire, you have already been told about. But there is also DONG, under General Samuels' command."

"DONG?"

"D-O-N-G," Unc Sam explained in more detail. "That's Defense *Of* National Guard."

"It's actually the plan that is most likely to be put into motion," Beardsley went on. "The plain fact of the matter is, of course, that no National Guard unit in the whole country is capable of protecting itself. DONG, then, is responsible for the safekeeping of the Guard. Just as General Admire would automatically be granted command of all US regular forces in the event of a National Guard coup, so would General Samuels automatically become the US supreme commander if it were necessary to come to the defense of the Guard."

"But I don't understand," Toby said. "Who would bother to attack the Guard?"

"A good question," Unc answered. "Obviously, the Russkies

or the Chinee or none of that crowd are going to bother harassing the National Guard. They've got bigger fish to fry. But some of the home-grown subversives might stoop that low."

"You must understand," Beardsley broke in, "that, practically speaking, the National Guard is defenseless. I spoke of our computer exercises with regard to DANG. Well, we have conducted similar hypothetical computer tests where the Guard was attacked by someone—and received no reinforcement from DONG."

"Yes?"

"Almost any organization that we programed into the computer could beat the Guard," Beardsley said.

"Let me see that list," Unc Sam cried, and Beardsley reached into his briefcase and handed the DONG chief a thick manila folder. "Here is the list of just some of the groups— American groups—who could defeat the National Guard in combat: the Mafia, of course; the Alabama State Police; the National Rifle Association; several of the nigger groups"— Unc licked his thumb and flipped through a number of pages —"the Hell's Angels; the Teamsters; the ladies' Roller Derby all-stars; the Benevolent and Protective Order of Elks; the Chicago Black Hawks; the Merv Griffin Fan Club; the Department of Health, Education, and Welfare; and so forth, and so on, etc., etc." Unc flipped with disgust through the rest of the folder. "Any one of them could beat the National Guard in combat."

"It would be no trick at all," Beardsley said sadly, shaking his head, "for one strong, clever man to tumble the whole Guard."

Toby whistled in amazement.

"I think you can see the sort of thing we're driving at, your alternative responsibility on this mission," Admire said. "Are you familiar with clichés, Major?" Toby said he was. "Good, I'm glad you have some expertise in that area, because now we're getting down to where the rubber hits the road. Let's see that photo."

Beardsley jiggled open a false bottom in his briefcase and pulled out a large glossy print. He handed it to Admire, who patted it proudly. "Take a good look at this man," he told Toby. "We want you to keep a close eye on him in Baltimore. He could be the major conspirator against the Maryland National Guard, or he could be in cahoots with someone even bigger, the country over. This man could be the key."

He threw the picture on the table in front of Toby, who leaned down to look at it carefully. His eyes popped, and he fell down upon it for closer examination. Then he drew back in shock. "Jesus Christ," Toby said. "I know him. He's my old buddy."

Certainly there was no doubt that that man was Jerry Start.

3

Wait till after
We View the Films

They all glared in disbelief at Toby. "You know him?" Unc Sam finally said.

"That's hard to believe," Admire gasped.

"I know it's hard to believe," Toby said. "It seems impossible to me that he could be tied up in a thing like this."

"No, it's not hard to believe anything these days," Admire said, patting Toby on the back as a measure of consolation.

"He's one of my very oldest friends," Toby said. "I went to school with him, I hung around with him, I played football with him. He even married an old girl friend of mine."

That brought forth a string of oaths from Samuels that were extreme even for him. Admire simply collapsed in his chair. Beardsley said, "He did?"

"I was like this with Jerry," Toby said, twisting the first two fingers on his right hand together. "And Rosalie too," he added rather unconsciously.

Suddenly, Admire jumped up and grabbed the picture from the table. "Hold it," he cried. "I see what's up. He's not talking about the nigger. Savvy? He's talking about the white guy with him."

"What nigger?" Toby said.

"This one," Admire said, pointing to the photograph. There was a well-dressed young black man standing next to Jerry Start in some kind of office. "What's your friend doing in this picture?"

"Well, I don't know," Toby said. "He's a stockbroker. Maybe this is his office."

"What firm is he with?"

"It's called Pine Brothers and Moore."

"Yeah, and so is that Negro," Beardsley said. "When our agent snapped this picture your buddy must of just been there. It's the Negro that will be your concern. He's head of a whole Baltimore battalion in the Maryland National Guard."

Toby looked at the photograph again and swallowed. "The colored guy is?"

Samuels said, "He's the real nigger in the woodpile—our woodpile."

"Still, strange as it seems, he appears to be a competent officer," Beardsley went on, assuming the briefing air. "His name is Tatler—Roosevelt Tatler. He's called Sandy. He's real slick. Somehow this Negro has gotten in with the whole white power structure of the city. The best financial people, businessmen, educators—they listen to him. His clients include some of the most influential people in the city of Baltimore, in the whole state.

"A fluke accident—maybe not an accident, huh?—and he ends up head of a whole battalion in the Guard at twenty-eight. Now that the guy in Cleveland pulled it off a couple weeks ago, he's thinking about running for mayor. And with the white support he's got, he's a shoo-in. Tatler could end up governor, senator. You want to know how powerful he is, Major? Tatler has got ten seats on the fifty-yard line at Colt games. Ten of the best seats, on the aisle, the fifty-yard line."

Toby whistled. "That's incredible."

"And nobody yet knows how he got those seats," Admire said.

"We've got the CIA working on it for us," Beardsley continued, "but even they've hit a dead end. How can a young man —a young Negro man at that—be so powerful that he can rate ten season tickets on the fifty-yard line of the Baltimore Colts? How, how?"

"It's hard to believe," Admire suggested.

"The CIA can trace those tickets back so far, to a bank president named Davis Tyler—"

"I remember him," Toby said. "He's about the biggest banker in Baltimore. Oldest family, richest—"

"Right," Beardsley said, "only he's been dead five years. Allegedly shot to death in a hunting accident."

"You mean murder?"

Beardsley shrugged. Admire came in: "Let's face it, the world-wide Communist conspiracy will use anything to get their dirty work done—women, drugs, liquor, bribery, blackmail. It is not inconceivable that now they own blocks of desirable pro football season tickets for the same purposes. Savvy?"

"I never thought of that," Toby admitted.

"We can't prove it," Beardsley said, "but we're pretty sure the Commies got bunches of tickets for pro football bought all over the country—New York, LA, right here in DC. Promise a guy good seats, he'll turn over a little microfilm, a little info, some blueprints."

"That's the way those rat bastards work," Unc Sam said.

Toby nodded and looked again at the black man in the photograph. "Ten Colt season tickets," Toby said. "What power the man has. I can't comprehend it."

"It is hard to believe," Admire said. "Now this old friend of yours in the picture—"

"Jerry Start."

"Yeah. I can assure you that it's only a coincidence that he's in the picture, but maybe a very provident coincidence. It might be good for you to renew old acquaintances with him. Are you familiar with Machiavelli, Major?" Toby said it rang a bell. "Well, good, it might be clever for you to get to know Tatler through this friend of yours."

"I'll call up Jerry tonight," Toby said.

"Good, and one last thing."

Beardsley took the cue and tossed another glossy photograph before Toby. It was a simple FBI mug shot. "Recognize him?"

"Sure," Toby said. "He's one of those colored guys. One of those militants."

"Right. That's Tyrone Dancer of the United Afro-American Alliance. He blew up a bunch of National Guard armories in California. Only by the grace of God, no one was even scratched. But then the sonofabitch put LSD in the canteens of a whole Guard division when it was alerted for riot duty. Then he stole all the rifles. Luckily for us, very few rifles in the National Guard work, or there would have been hell to pay."

"We almost had to call DONG into action," Unc Sam said.

"Dancer escaped," Beardsley went on. "We know he's just missed getting out of the country three times—the last time on a freighter out of Baltimore. We know he didn't make it, but his trail went dead there back in August, and get this— that was just about the time Tatler took over the Guard. Just a coincidence?"

Unc Sam guffawed. "Are you familiar with the law of averages, Major?" Admire said. "You see, we're not saying that Tatler knows where Dancer is hiding, but DANG and DONG will not take any chances. We've had a full-time undercover agent on the scene for a couple of months just waiting for Tatler to lead us to Dancer."

"Will I know who the agent is?" Toby asked.

"Soon enough," Beardsley replied. "But we can't tell you when. That we've got to leave up to the agent. You'll know who it is when you see the code word flashed to you."

"What's the code word?"

Beardsley opened the false bottom again and pulled out a sheet of green paper. It had one word printed on it, in red and in heavy block letters. The word was: OVERLORD.

"Overlord?" Toby said.

"Right."

"But that was the word for D-Day."

"Stick with a winner," Unc said.

"I'll remember it," Toby assured them all.

"Well, don't worry about it," Beardsley said. "Contact is the agent's business. Your primary task is to play football and to try to keep an eye on Tatler." He put another folder down on the table. "That's Tatler's file. There's not much hard data in it, but read it carefully before you leave."

"Yes sir," Toby said, and he began to study the papers, looking for the one clue that might help him understand how any one man could control ten fifty-yard-line Colt tickets. Of course he could divine nothing, for, like DANG and DONG and the CIA, Toby was going at it all backward. He was ignoring the reverse possibility—*not* that Sandy Tatler had the tickets because he was something special, but that he had become something special because he had the tickets. In ignorance he went back to his billet to call the Starts.

4

Reading the Defenses

Jerry had known Toby long before he ever met Rosalie. Toby was a year ahead of Jerry in school, but they got to know each other on the football team, and then Toby let Jerry hang around with him, watching him squeeze the life out of beer cans and things such as that. Toby was always hot stuff, and Jerry stood in awe of him. Toby just said, "No sweat," to whatever came up, and that is the way it worked out for him. Even after *he* married Rosalie, Jerry remained jealous of Toby.

When Toby called Jerry up at the office Monday as soon as he had driven up to Baltimore, Jerry started talking loudly in the hopes that everybody else would hear who he was talking to. "Toby, Toby Geyser, you old sonofagun," he yelled. "How 'bout coming over tomorrow night? We'll get some of the old gang over."

"Great."

"No, wait, Tobe. Tomorrow is my Guard night. How 'bout Wednesday?"

"Sure," said Toby.

At times like this it never occurred to Jerry that Rosalie should be consulted. That was because at times like this Jerry would forget that Rosalie was part of the picture. It was just as if it were only he and Toby, back in Towson High together, sneaking into Timonium Racetrack in the guise of newsboys, or hanging around the Towson Teen Center trying to come up with bare tit. Rosalie just didn't fit in with Jerry *and* Toby; or, if she fitted in at all, it was just with Toby. Jerry had never even met Rosalie until she was already established as Toby's girl.

She was a freshman then, and Toby was a junior. Jerry had seen Rosalie around before, but the day Toby introduced her to him she was a different person altogether. This was because she was one of those girls who grew up overnight; also, Toby was one of those rare guys who knew enough to be there on hand the morning after a girl grew up overnight. Rosalie came to school that particular morning, and all of a sudden she had her hair done right and she had good boobs and she knew how to cradle her books and wear socks. The day before she had possessed none of this.

Toby spotted her right away and walked over to the group Rosalie was standing in. All the other girls either froze or started babbling compulsively. Rosalie just held her ground, shifting her tits. Toby walked up to her and said, "Hi, I'm Toby Geyser." And then he waited.

Now, under the rules of conduct there were exactly three things that Rosalie could choose to do. One, she could giggle. Two, she could say, "Toby who?" which would be *a real scream*, since every girl at Towson knew quite well who Toby Geyser was. Or three, she could be wise and say, "Big deal." Those were the three accepted possible replies in a case like this.

Rosalie looked Toby in the eye, gave him a nice big smile, and said, "Gee, hi, Tony, I'm Rosalie Totter." Get it: Tony, not Toby. He was dumfounded. He didn't have any routine to work off that. He just stood there trying to think of something to say until the morning bell rang. Rosalie smiled brightly again and walked past him, taking a wide berth. When everyone else was gone, Reds Ritchie rapped Toby on his bicep and said, "Squelched, man." The story was all over school by the first lunch period, and when Toby finally did recover sufficiently to call Rosalie up the next night for a date, he still did not feel confident enough to ask her out to the drive-in. He made it a point to specify the Towson, which was just a regulation theater.

By the time Toby introduced Jerry to Rosalie in the cafeteria a few days later, she was already recognized as his steady. Jerry's first impression, not necessarily an exaggerated one, was that Rosalie surely must be the best-looking girl at Towson, or possibly in all of Baltimore County. This opinion was shortly affirmed by her inclusion on the school cheerleading squad and on the Hutzler's department store teen modeling panel. Furthermore, she could dance better than any girl in existence, although Jerry may have been somewhat biased in this conclusion by the fact that whenever she did dance it drew her McMullen blouse tight across her chest and actually permitted an observer (such as Jerry) to perceive the outline of her bra cups.

When Toby finally went away to West Point and he and Rosalie broke up and Jerry later started taking her out, he worked it so that there was never any possibility that he and Rosalie would end up near a dance floor. Just in case, he also developed a much-discussed (if nonexistent) trick knee, which always acted up at dance time. Jerry could not even manage a very good "close dance," because he could never figure out where to shove his hard-on in his chinos, and people such as Reds Ritchie would invariably spot his predicament and call out such things as, "I'm wise to the rise in your Levis."

And then, besides everything else, Toby was also the dance sensation of the nation. He could rock, cha-cha, samba, close dance, you name it. He and Rosalie could even waltz. Toby could do just about everything important well, so when he went off to West Point and left Rosalie behind, everybody was intimidated by his memory. When Jerry ran across Rosalie in the corridors, he wouldn't even dare talk to her about anything that had to do with boys and girls together—that is, about parties or movies or the Top Forty, that sort of thing. Instead, he would choose subjects like teachers or the Colts that could not even remotely suggest to her that he was even aware of her gender. Then Jerry would go home and beat off like a fury in her honor.

Rosalie was going out of her mind. She had had only two dates the whole year. One was a creepy blind date from Towson Catholic that a friend fixed her up with, and the other was a guy she had met at the beach that summer who drove up from Washington. He had looked much better in a Madras bathing suit and a tan. In December he appeared in powder-blue pegged pants and a one-button roll, revealing himself immediately as a real greaser.

Nonetheless, what really worried Rosalie was that she readily agreed to go with him to the drive-in and let him get outside second base before the first feature was halfway along. It was a whole minute or so before it suddenly dawned on her that she was actually turning into a slut. "What are you, Italian?" Rosalie cried, yanking away from him. "You've sure got roamin' hands."

"What is this fake-out?" the poor greaser said, completely bewildered at this sudden turn of events.

"Take me right home," Rosalie said. She did not trust herself. She was scared she was going to let the guy give her another first-class feel if they stayed. "I mean it. You're cruisin' for a bruisin'."

"Okay, okay," the greaser said. "Don't go ape. Okay."

"Just because you're from Washington, you think you're a real MOA, don't you?" Rosalie went on. She wouldn't let up.

"Okay, okay. Big deal."

She left his car and ran into the house, crying, while he peeled out, leaving rubber on the road as a signature.

The brief interlude only made it worse for Rosalie, and her social life did not improve at Towson. Nobody was anxious to be the act that followed Toby Geyser. "Look at that," Reds Ritchie said during a time-out in a basketball game when Rosalie was throwing her fanny all around, leading the cheers: give me a T, give me an O, and so on. "Almost every guy in the stands has got a hard-on."

"Don't give me any of that jazz," Jerry said. "You'd like to be in her pants too, Reds."

"No way," Reds said emphatically. "How's that grab you?"

"Who are you kidding, Dick Tracy?"

"After Tobe dipped his wick in, I wouldn't want any sloppy seconds."

"'Cause she'd say you were sloppy," Johnny Parker said. "You spastic."

"Fuckin' A, you weenie," Reds said. "I'm not in Tobe's league."

"You really think he went all the way with her?" said Cholly Messerschmidt. He was kind of a fringe guy in the group, trying to break in as a regular.

"Christ, Messerschmidt, are you out to lunch," Johnny Parker said.

"Duhhhhh," said Jerry. "Grow up."

"Well, she was only a sophomore," Cholly said.

"It's about your friends, Parker," Herbie Hood said. Cholly's patron in the group was Johnny Parker.

"Eat it on a stick," Johnny said.

"Stop hacking around and get a load of that," Reds said.

Rosalie was finishing the cheer with one of those spread-eagle moves, where her legs ended up stretched out in completely different directions all over the floor. "A girl can't even do that if she's still got her maidenhead. That's no shit."

"Fuckin' A," Jerry said.

As it was, Jerry never got up enough nerve to ask Rosalie out that year, his last one at Towson. Then, by chance, when he came back for Christmas vacation the next year from the University of Maryland, he ran across her in the Towson Plaza, by the escalators. With all the Santa Clauses around and the Muzak carols, it seemed different, more of a family atmosphere than a boy-girl thing, so he casually asked her—sort of for old times' sake, you understand—to come along to a little party he was going to that evening with some of his new college friends. Jerry was very brotherly-and-sisterly with Rosalie, and he didn't lay a hand near her, never mind on her, all night.

However, giddy with her proximity and the large amounts of cheap beer that he had consumed at the party, Jerry lost complete control of himself as they drove up in front of Rosalie's house, and before he realized what a fool he was making of himself, he asked her out for New Year's Eve. That was sheer madness on his part, because at that time New Year's Eve was the most crucial date on any young person's social calendar. To tacitly admit, as Jerry was, that here it was December 22, and he did not yet have anyone committed to him for New Year's Eve, stamped him as an outcast of the first water.

Everybody, boy or girl, started pointing for New Year's Eve in November, or even October, if you were still psychologically scarred from a failure the previous December 31. Nobody ever broke up with anybody from Thanksgiving on, at the risk of not being paired up for sure on that magic evening. That generation's inclination for playing it safe, for security and conformity, derives directly from the traumatic pressures associated with

New Year's Eve. Studies at both Duke University and Sacramento State College have firmly established this link. It was shocking enough for Jerry to be asking any girl out for New Year's Eve as late as December 22, but in the case of someone as gorgeous and popular as Rosalie, it was insane for Jerry to but think that—

5

Real Physical

"Great, I'd love to," Rosalie said straightaway, a reply that so discombobulated Jerry that he somehow got his arm entangled in the steering wheel and started blowing the horn.

The fact is, Rosalie certainly did already have a date for New Year's Eve. For that matter, so did Jerry. Nobody took any chances. Rosalie was scheduled to go out with a pipe-smoking sophomore from Johns Hopkins, whose only edge was that he was going to take her to the party at the St. A's fraternity house. Jerry, having swallowed his pride, had finally lined up Carla Poole.

She was his old reliable, having inducted him into manhood one summer night in her club cellar on what she called a "divan." On times like this New Year's, when he was desperate, he would ask her out again, although normally he would try not to stray far from the divan with her. There was something of a social price to be paid for being seen in her company. Carla was maligned by the expression "everyone into the Poole," and she had a habit of hanging around the Towson practice field and permitting the football-players to give her a quick passing feel for luck. As a consequence, she was often distinguished by a dirty blouse.

But Jerry could not be choosy, even though relations with Carla were further strained because she was Roman Catholic and, like all Catholic girls, was always conscious of where French kissing could deposit her soul in the great by-and-by. Jerry would invariably forget himself and get the old tongue working again just when he was ready to score on the divan. This meant that Carla had to call a halt to everything, cross her bare breasts, and require a cooling-off period.

He desperately needed more of that kind of problem, but, with Rosalie suddenly in tow, he called Carla up and explained that his parents were forcing him to go with them over New Year's when they visited his sister Betty at Otis Air Force Base in Massachusetts, where her husband was stationed. For her part, Rosalie called up the pipe-smoker and, double-talking about a debilitating malady that was "going around the family," broke their date. Then Rosalie went out and bought the most beautiful party dress she could find, and shoes and a purse to go with it. She bought these things expressly for New Year's Eve, which would have stunned Jerry beyond belief had he only known.

Unfortunately, though, buying things for New Year's Eve and buying things for Jerry were somewhat different. Actually, Jerry was being taken for a patsy. Rosalie had learned from a friend who had heard it from the best pal of the guy who double-dated with Reds Ritchie's sister that Toby Geyser might be stopping over in Baltimore on New Year's Eve on his way back to West Point from Florida. His parents had retired to Port Charlotte after he went to the Academy. Rosalie had heard this rumor, as a matter of fact, on December 22, the very day Jerry happened to ask her out for New Year's Eve.

As New Year's at Reds' house wore on, however, and Rosalie learned that Toby Geyser was not returning, Jerry's witticisms and even his rendition of a close dance began to look better and better to Rosalie. A great deal of rum and Coke may have influenced this drift of her mind, but when he bent over, tentatively, for the obligatory midnight kiss, she reached up and pulled him down to her by the neck and kissed him a great deal better than Carla Poole ever had. They didn't go around and kiss everybody else then, like all the others, but stayed wrapped in each other's arms. "It's 1960, Jerry," Rosalie whispered. "The 1950s are all gone." And in that instant, unbeknownst to each other, they both had the same strange sensation, that is: that the other had blue hair, just like in all the true-love comic strips. Obviously, they were meant for each other.

As if by magnetic force they left and headed for Parton's, an old deserted horse farm off Joppa Road, where everybody from Towson went to make out—park at Parton's. Jerry was in a daze. He got to inside second base.

. . . and their love blossomed . . .

He would commute home from college every weekend to see her. By February, Reds Ritchie knew enough to stop saying "sloppy seconds" every time he saw Jerry. Later that month Jerry and Rosalie began saying, "I love you," and, "I love you too." By Easter, they spoke authoritatively of eternal love, although in Jerry's eyes her claims were somewhat clouded by the fact that she had avoided the business of going to bed with him. Alone, he would curse her and call her the most incredible names, most of them relating to the known fact that she had "fucked like a bunny" for Toby Geyser. At last Jerry resolved to settle the matter once and for all.

He came back to see her one weekend when his parents were away in Massachusetts visiting Betty. Jerry picked Rosalie up and, dispensing with the usual who-shot-John, returned her immediately to the empty house, in order, he explained, that they might "play some 45s." Nonetheless, despite a real bed, yawning like the Memorial Stadium outfield in comparison to the usual front seat of his green-and-silver Chevy Bel Air, Rosalie was as reluctant as ever to give in. She rolled to the side of the bed and turned sideways, away from Jerry, every time he tried to pull her Bermudas down. "No, no, not here, Jerry," she said.

"Don't you love me?"

"I've told you I love you. You know I love you. I'm just not ready to do the deed."

Suddenly, Jerry could not keep it to himself any more. "You really love him, don't you?"

"Love who?" Rosalie said, knowing damn well who.

"Toby."

She sat up so fast in bed, turning in anger at the same time, that the breast closest to him flung around and actually stung him in the face. It really smarted. "Ow," he said.

"Is that what you think? I haven't seen Toby in over a year and a half," Rosalie cried, and her whole body was taut in anger. Jerry didn't know what more to say. "More than a year and a half. It will be two years in June," Rosalie went on. She was firm on the dates.

"Well, you know," Jerry said defensively, before he knew he had actually said it, "you could do it with Toby, so I don't see why—"

"Do what?"

"You know."

"Jerry, I'm a virgin," Rosalie cried. "We never did the deed. You thought I did the deed with Toby. Did Toby ever say—"

"No, no, Toby never—"

"Well, what made you think—"

"Well, for Chrissakes, you went out with him for two years, for Chrissakes, for two whole years almost."

"Well, I don't care if it was a hundred years, I never did. I'm no slut," Rosalie said. She was mad as hell, and crying a little on the side for effect, but Jerry didn't even bother to chase after her when she ran from the room. He was flabbergasted. It was like finding out one of the big he-man movie stars was a fag. Also, it put a whole new slant on things. Not only did it make Rosalie all the more desirable, but now, if he ever did get to screw her, she could not compare him with Toby.

Rosalie finally did give in to Jerry late that summer. It happened the day after Jerry at last learned to do the twist without using a towel. They were down at the beach in Ocean City, staying with Jack "the Hacker" Webster and his date, and his parents, all of whom were out crabbing. Jerry was so pleased with himself that he put Chubby Checker on and started twisting with Rosalie. Suddenly, without warning, Rosalie just started unzipping her bathing suit, right as they twisted, and mumbling something about doing the deed. She took him by the hand and led him to a bedroom. Jerry was alternately so confused and excited that he neglected to take his own bathing suit off, an oversight which somewhat marred the aesthetics of things when at last it came to his attention.

After that, inasmuch as Rosalie had sacrificed herself to Jerry, it was understood that they would soon be married. Officially, he proposed to her in September. He was down in Virginia, visiting her at Sweet Briar for a weekend and when he called her up Sunday morning, before coming over to her dormitory to pick her up again, she said that she had gotten sick.

"You're not pregnant, are you?" Jerry whispered into the phone.

"Oh, no, honey, you know I just had the curse. It must be a bug or something. I'll be okay."

"All right, Baby Cakes, just stay in bed and read the Sunday paper and take it easy."

"Right, that's exactly what I'm doing," Rosalie said, and Jerry drove back to Maryland. He called her up that night, and she reported that she had enjoyed a miraculous recovery and would even be able to attend classes the next day. Jerry ventured that it might have been something that she had eaten. Then, on Tuesday, Jerry got a letter from Rosalie. Since they spoke to each other on the phone constantly and saw each other at every chance, a letter was obviously something special, so Jerry put it in his pocket and walked over to his room at the SAE house, where he could read it in complete privacy.

He seated himself in a chair, turned Rosalie's picture around to face him, and opened the letter, which Rosalie had dated 11 a.m., Sunday. It began, "My dearest darling Jerry, I do love you so much . . ." and it went on from there, detailing every possible aspect of that love, and the likelihood, impossible as it seemed, that that love would grow and multiply. The letter concluded with a presentation of the agonies that beset her when he was not close by her side. Jerry was overwhelmed. Even he had never given himself quite this much credit. He made plans to take a quick trip down to Sweet Briar later that afternoon to respond personally and propose.

Following this interlude, Jerry reached for the morning paper and turned to the sports section for a break in the reverie. There were two large headlines: PIRATES' MAGIC NUMBER DOWN TO SIX and 'SKINS GEAR FOR EAGLE AERIAL GAME. Down from the latter, his eye caught another smaller headline. It read:

TAB ARMY STAR
BACK OF WEEK

Jerry began reading:

The Associated Press' first Back of the Week honors have been awarded to Army Halfback Toby Geyser for his performance Saturday against Wake Forest. The junior sensation was a one-man juggernaut in leading the Cadets to a 41–7 rout of the Deacons in the season's lidlifter for both elevens.

Geyser, a powerful 6'2", 195-pound speedster from Towstown [sic], Md., scored four touchdowns on runs of 11, 27, and 64 yards from scrimmage, and 93 yards on the kickoff that opened the second half. Moreover, he threw for another TD on a rare halfback pass play. Overall, he raced for 209 yards from scrimmage.

Geyser, who sat out almost all of his sophomore season with a bout of mononucleosis, made up for lost time. He showed that the Black Knights of the Hudson have another bona fide All-American backfield candidate in the tradition of Glenn Davis, Doc Blanchard, and Pete Dawkins.

Scout Jed Trumbull of the Buffalo Bills of the AFL said, "Geyser is good enough right now to start with any team in either pro league. I know the boy has a service obligation to his country, but I still think he'll go high in the draft next year. Some team will have to gamble. A talent like Geyser comes along only once every generation!"

Jerry put the paper down and said, "Up yours, Tobe." Then, chuckling, he left for the ride to Sweet Briar to propose. It never occurred to him that the original accounts of the Army–Wake Forest game, with Toby's exploits explained at length, would have appeared in the Sunday papers and might have terribly upset someone who had almost forgotten him.

Nor, for that matter, did Jerry read any significance into the fact that Rosalie took to her bed with strange headaches the day, years later, when the papers reported that Major Geyser had been wounded in courageous combat in War Zone C.

6

Good Field Position

Most mornings Jerry was sluggish getting up and into Pine Brothers and Moore, Brokers. The word that Toby was coming back to Baltimore kept him tossing much of the night, though, and at last he gave up and roused himself early from bed and went out and picked up the *Morning Sun*, so that he could read all the locker-room accounts of yesterday's win over the Rams.

At almost the same time, a few miles away in Baltimore, in a red-brick development named Far Lake Estates, Sandy Tatler slipped on his wrapper and hustled outside to get his paper. He was every bit as much a pro football maniac as Jerry was. Pro football is no respecter of race, color, or creed. Sandy lingered over every word about the game, memorized the standings, and at last, beaming, pulled out of his driveway in his brand-new 1968 Oldsmobile 98 and started driving downtown to work. From Far Lake Estates, Sandy was required to drive through Guilford, one of the best, most fashionable white sections of the city, and a few people who saw him go by raised their fists and screamed at him. He honked his horn at them and waved back. Sandy had a huge COLT HEAVEN IN '67 sticker that ran the full length of his bumper, and the day after such a great win as the Colts had enjoyed over Los Angeles, everyone who spotted the sticker signaled in delight.

In the rush-hour traffic along St. Paul Street, people rolled down their windows at stoplights and called to each other, "How about those Colts?" and, "Yea, Johnny U!" Sandy made such snap replies as, "All the way," and, "Go to war, Miss Agnes." The cop at the Saratoga Street intersection made a TD sign for Sandy, raising his arms overhead, and at the parking lot all the attendants rushed to take Sandy's car so that they would have a chance to chat with him about the game. At the Read's soda fountain, where he picked up some coffee, he and the take-out clerk compared their views of the more stirring plays. "That nigger has seats on the fifty-yard line," the clerk told the cashier girl after Sandy left.

Outside, striding along happily, his overcoat thrown open to the unusually pleasant weather, Sandy walked down Redwood Street and into the Gothic old building that housed the Gothic old firm of Pine Brothers and Moore. Jerry was there already, standing at the switchboard, trying to look down the dress of Miss Chickie Pendleton, the gorgeous receptionist from Glen Burnie with the raven hair and the grating nasal accent.

"Gamorn'n', Sandy," Chickie said.

"Would you believe the Super Bowl for the Hosses?" Jerry said.

"Go to war, Miss Agnes," Sandy replied.

Only on Mondays was Jerry in the office so early. That was because he was required to take a great deal of time off in the middle of every Monday to attend the Colt Stampede luncheon. There he would watch film highlights and meet with other

Colt Stampeders. Sometimes real ex-Colts showed up to speak. Jerry won his Lenny Lyles–Ordelle Braase autographed regulation football as a door prize there once too. The Stampede luncheon consumed much of Jerry's working day, and he felt quite guilty about it until he learned one day that the firm's Wall Street representative was himself away from the office from noon until three every Monday, attending similar booster-club ceremonies in honor of the Giants at a fancy midtown Manhattan restaurant.

Jerry, like Rosalie, like all the people in all the cities like Baltimore all over the country, was dazzled by anything that came out of New York, from the Johnny Carson Show on up. What really convinced Jerry that he should go into selling stocks was that stocks are New York. Consequently, Jerry would begin most conversations with clients by declaring, "New York says . . ."—as in, "New York says buy," or, "New York says sell," or, "New York says sit tight for a while."

As it was always some time each morning before the earliest word came down from New York, Jerry found the beginning of each day the most convenient time to spend peering down Chickie's front. Since Jerry was tall, with a natural vantage, he presumed, like most tall men, that he was adroit at looking down fronts without giving himself away. Inasmuch as Chickie could never find any clothes to conceal her heaving breasts adequately, however, Jerry's height gave him no great edge in this case. Chickie had served as quite a morale-booster for the office ever since she had arrived a couple of months ago to take over the switchboard.

Of course, she did exhibit a frightful Baltimore accent, that awful twang common to many residents of the mid-Atlantic states, where Brooklynese, Pennsylvania Dutch, and hillbilly mesh into one dialect that assaults any unaccustomed ear. If, for instance, Chickie delivered this message: "Ah dolled yur hame phane, but yur buoy had leff wid the koor to govda the Balamer Street druckstore," only a student familiar with the strange tongue would know that she had said: "I dialed your home phone, but your boy had left with the car to go over to the Baltimore Street drugstore." In Chickie's case, however, it was possible to overlook this deficiency because of the cleavage. Chickie was the only person in the world that Jerry permitted to call him "Jer." He detested the name, but, as he had explained to Chickie once, at old Rip Sprinkles' retirement party: "Baby Cakes, you can call me anything but late for dinner."

Any day after a big game, Jerry limited his time with Chickie, since he felt that there was so much required talking about the game that he was obligated to participate in with his fellow fans. So, with a last fond peer, he left her and headed back to his desk. Sandy sat in the cubicle next to Jerry's. They were separated by a frosted-glass partition, although joined by a hole in the partition where their Quotemaster machine was located. That is the machine which reveals the latest stock quotations, which the broker can summon up merely by punching the key buttons. Brokers at Pine Brothers and Moore had to share Quotemasters, one for each two cubicles, and the luck of the draw had matched Jerry and Sandy.

Well, perhaps it was not just coincidence. The two young men shared three very important experiences in their lives—Pine Brothers and Moore, the National Guard, and Colt season tickets—and while these elements seemed so diverse that not even DANG and DONG had pieced them together, the fact is that they were all significantly intertwined.

Certainly the Colts were bond enough. As soon as Jerry reached his desk, Sandy peered through the Quotemaster opening and began a Simulated Conversation with Jerry about the previous day's game. Simulated Conversations are the kind pro football fans participate in, the country over. They may seem logical in their progression but in fact, nothing said in a Simulated Conversation has any direct relationship with what precedes it or what follows. Rosalie always felt that pro football Simulated Conversations were reminiscent of the dialogue on an old radio program that was called *It Pays to Be Ignorant*.

On this show, there were a moderator and some panelists, who were presumed to be dimwits. For instance, the moderator would say, "The first question is: what color was George Washington's white horse?" One panelist would immediately answer, "My Uncle Fred used to own horses," and another would say, "I went to Washington on the train last summer," and a third would say, "I don't think it's fair to always put the caboose at the end of the train," and it would go on and on like that, while the studio audience laughed its ass off. The only difference with pro football Simulated Conversations is that nobody laughs and many more people are the panelists.

Warming up, Jerry said, "This Colt team does not have as much talent as some others, but it is all heart."

Sandy said, "Exactly. A rookie in the defensive backfield is worth at least one touchdown every game."

Jerry replied, "That's right, our linebackers turned it around with their stunting."

Sandy added, "Of course, that was the best post pattern I ever saw Richardson run against the Ram secondary."

Jerry said, "Yessir, old Johnny U."

Sandy said, "Sure, our splits seemed too large, but it made them go further on the routes."

Jerry replied, "And then they were surprising us with the quick counts."

Sandy said, "The set offense is too complex for a man to learn in a week, but Toby Geyser could be a real plus on the suicide squads against the Packers."

This remark—Toby's name—dented Jerry's consciousness,

and he responded as he would in a real conversation. He said, "You know, Toby called us up last night."

Sandy said, "The way I saw it, on the flares and play-action we were looping instead of sticking with the safety blitz."

Jerry went on. "Yeah, Toby and I played together in high school. One game his last year, Sandy, he ran for three touchdowns and passed for three more—and I caught two of them."

Sandy peered in through the Quotemaster opening and said, "What?" He was late in coming around, because he understood this to be strictly a Simulated Conversation.

Jerry said, "You know—Toby Geyser. When I played with Toby."

Sandy said, "You played with Toby Geyser?"

"Well, that's what I just got through saying, Sandy. In high school, at Towson. He was a tailback and I was an end. Single wing."

"Did you really know him?"

"Hey, weren't you listening? I just said he called me up last night. He called me before it was on television or anything."

"I'll be a sonofabitch," Sandy said.

"Hell, Toby used to take Rosalie out in high school," Jerry went on.

"I'll be damned," Sandy exclaimed. In all the time he had known Sandy, Jerry had never before felt so impressive in his presence. Sometimes Jerry forgot that Toby Geyser was such a mythic figure that merely being his old buddy was sufficient to stun some people. Sooner or later everybody would ask, "What is Toby Geyser really like, really?" And since Sandy appeared on the verge of that, Jerry was glad that his phone rang.

Normally he was reluctant to discuss business at this early hour, because the word had not come down yet from New York pertaining to what stocks to buy or to sell or to sit tight on. This time, however, to escape discussing what Toby was really like, Jerry was glad to pick up the phone. To help him in a blind spot like this, he always listened to the early-morning stock summary on the car radio. Thus Jerry could say things like, "It appears the market is mixed in moderate trading," or, "The market is keeping a wary eye on Washington developments," with promises to call back later in the day.

This system invariably worked out, because whenever it was later in the day, the market had gone up some more. The whole time Jerry had been selling stocks, everything always went up. Oh, the Dow Jones might dip down a teeny-weeny bit every now and then, but, as they always took pains to explain on the radio, these little drops were merely "technical readjustments" that the market was making. Whenever the market went down, it was a technical readjustment; whenever it went up, it was something else altogether again, like a boom. This made stockbroker a good job to have around 1967.

Notwithstanding this general situation, Jerry was dismayed this particular morning to discover that his first caller was none other than Fewster C.P. Benton IV, the very person who had put Jerry onto the hottest stock ever. Jerry always liked to be especially alert for Fewster C.P. Benton IV. Luckily, he had heard the radio stock forecast and was able to say real fast, "Well, as I understand it, large investors are remaining on the sidelines, searching for bargains in year-end profit-taking."

Benton thanked Jerry for this inside dope, and then, naturally, they fell into a long Simulated Conversation. It was much the same as the one that Jerry had participated in only moments before with Sandy, and some of Sandy's comments had lodged in Jerry's unconscious, and now he played them back for Fewster C.P. Benton IV. That is the way it works with these things. Simulated Conversations contain a more selective level of jargon as any week wears on.

In the instance of the upcoming Green Bay game, Jerry and all good fans had less time to perfect their art. The college football season had ended, and thus, for TV purposes, the Packers and Colts were scheduled a day early, on Saturday instead of Sunday. That put the pressure on the fans. As soon as Fewster C.P. Benton IV rang off, Jerry called Chickie at the switchboard. "Hold my phones for a while, will you, Baby Cakes?" he said. "I have some important studying to do."

"You got it, Jer," she rasped. Then Jerry closed his door, made sure that Sandy was not peeking in past the Quotemaster, and reached into his desk and pulled out several sporting magazines and newspapers and a special mimeographed newsletter that came, at substantial cost, direct from New York every week. It was entitled *Expert Pro Grid*, and it was written, Jerry understood, by two clever Chinese twins who were in on all the inside dope. These Chinese twins knew airline stewardesses who had contacts on every team in both leagues. Jerry was one of the few people in Baltimore to know of this dope sheet, much less receive it. He began to study it assiduously.

Next door, Sandy closed himself in, called Chickie, and told her to hold all his calls. Then he reached deep into his bottom desk drawer and pulled out several sports magazines and newspapers, and, as well, a special mimeographed newsletter that came every week direct from New York. It was an expensive item, but well worth it, because it contained valuable inside pro football information. Sandy had learned that this material had been obtained by the editor, who was actually a homosexual barber who was the confidant of many players, officials, and referees in both leagues. The journal was entitled *Expert Pro Grid*, and Sandy was one of the few people in Baltimore to have such a valuable pipeline, one that assured that he would stand out in any Simulated Conversation.

Just the chance to think about the Colts was delight enough for Sandy, however, for he owed the Colts more than any other man in the city of Baltimore. The Colts and pro football had made Sandy all that he was, and he never forgot that.

7

Play Action

Years before, in the summer before his senior year at Dunbar High School, Sandy had mailed in an application to the Colts for a season ticket. In those days, just before the Colts won their first championship, a few seats for the season were still available in the far reaches of the stadium. So Sandy applied for his season ticket: for R. Tatler. By dumb luck, a happenstance that would be bedeviling the likes of DONG, DANG, and the CIA a decade later, that very same day a powerful member of the Baltimore Board of Estimates named Ronald Taylor applied for ten season tickets. Taylor was a very important man, inasmuch as any improvements to the stadium would have to have his approval. The word filtered down from the Colt executives to move heaven and earth to get Ronald Taylor—or simply R. Taylor, as it said on his application—ten very good seats. Well, yes, that is exactly what happened: some dumb bunny in the ticket office mixed up R. Taylor and R. Tatler.

Believe it or not.

Sandy opened his letter from the Colts and saw that he had been allocated ten seats—not just the one he had requested— and that they were smack-dab on the fifty-yard line in Section 10, just far enough back to get a perfect view of the whole field and yet to also be under the protective cover of the overhanging upper deck. He had the best ten seats in the house.

Sandy's first inclination was to mail the form back, pointing out the error. For one thing, he didn't have $300 to pay for ten tickets; it was going to be enough just to scratch and save the $30 for one. But, Sandy thought, if he called attention to this error he would end up with a bad seat way up somewhere in Section 37. Then, in the next instant, he figured out something that was to send him on his way forever.

He put on his charcoal-gray suit and his pork-pie hat with the feather in it and went down the street until he reached the only bank he knew, the Pennsylvania Avenue branch of the First Merchants Trust. He asked the first friendly face he saw there —which belonged to a seventy-six-year-old messenger boy—who the president of the bank was. The old messenger boy laughed in his face and took him over to Jimmy O'Brien, who was the assistant manager of the bank. Jimmy laughed to beat the band when he heard that this little colored boy wanted to see Mr. Davis Tyler himself.

"Mr. Davis Tyler?" Sandy said, picking up the name.

"Davis Tyler," O'Brien answered, still chuckling. "But boy, you go down there, your ass is grass."

"I've got important business," Sandy said. "Where will I find this Mr. Davis Tyler?"

"The First Merchants Trust Building, right there on Calvert Street," O'Brien replied. He had already started thinking how funny it would be when they started screaming at this uppity nigger down at the main office, so he told Sandy exactly where Mr. Tyler's office was located. As soon as Sandy left, O'Brien called down to his friend at the main office, Boots Timberlake in the Christmas Club Department, and told him to watch out for the fireworks when this little colored boy marched in and tried to see the old man himself. Boots said he would call right back and tell him all about what happened.

Armed with Jimmy O'Brien's floor plan, however, Sandy sauntered right past all sorts of guards, right past Boots Timberlake, and right up the stairs to the executive offices on the mezzanine. Everybody just assumed that he was a particularly well-groomed messenger boy. Sandy took a left at the end of the hall, just as Jimmy O'Brien had told him to, and sure enough, there on the frosted glass of the open door it said L. DAVIS TYLER, PRESIDENT AND CHAIRMAN OF THE BOARD. There was one elderly white gentleman sitting there in the anteroom, but Sandy assumed this must be the office itself and the white man must be Davis Tyler. "Mr. Tyler?" he inquired.

Before the man answered, Sandy heard a voice behind him saying, "May I help you?" He turned around, and there was Mr. Tyler's secretary, Miss Mary Pratt, who was a bossy old lady with a distracting facial tic and a penchant for chain-smoking three packs of Hit Parade cigarettes a day.

"I'd like to see Mr. Davis Tyler," Sandy said, and then he remembered he still had his pork-pie hat on, and, sheepishly, he pulled it off his head.

"Do you have an appointment?" Miss Mary said, knowing damn well he didn't, and moving the left corner of her lip in such a way that Sandy was frightened a little.

"No ma'am. This just come up this morning."

"Well, Mr. Tyler is a very busy man, of course," Miss Mary said. "Perhaps, if you tell me the nature of your business, we can arrange an appointment with someone in the bank at some future time."

"Ma'am, I have to see Mr. Davis Tyler, and I have to see him today."

"Well, I'm afraid that is out of the question," Miss Mary said, getting snippy for the first time and blowing smoke in Sandy's face. Up to now, she figured she had been pretty damned patient with this boy. "How did you get in here anyway? And just what is the nature of your business?"

"I can only tell him that, ma'am."

"Well, if you can't tell me, I can't tell Mr. Tyler," Miss Mary said. She moved her foot over behind her desk to a buzzer and pushed it to signal a guard. The man waiting there, who was Shipley Pine, president of Pine Brothers and Moore, Brokers, noticed that Miss Mary was in some distress, and so he stood up. "May I help, Miss Mary?" he asked.

"I'm afraid this boy won't tell me the nature of his business."

"Oh."

"It's personal, sir. I have to see Mr. Davis Tyler himself."

"Have you ever met Mr. Tyler? Does he know you?" Pine asked, but kindly.

"No sir," Sandy said. "This just come up." A guard appeared, cast a menacing look at Sandy, and would have no doubt grabbed him and ushered him out straightaway, except that Shipley Pine appeared to be in charge.

"Well, if the matter is as important as you say it is, I'm sure Mr. Tyler would take the time to consider it if you left a note explaining what you have in mind. I'll deliver it to him myself. That's a promise," Pine said, a revelation that caused Miss Mary's tic to start up again at a furious pace.

"Yes sir," Sandy said. "Yes sir." Pine ordered Miss Mary to get him a pencil and some paper.

"You see, son," he said, "no matter how important your business is, Mr. Tyler could not possibly see you. Right now he is on an urgent long-distance phone call to New York, and then I have an appointment with him, and then he is having a business luncheon with some members of the Federal Reserve at the Maryland Club. But I'll give him your note, and you call back later in the day. You see, there is just no way he could find time to talk with you now. President Eisenhower himself couldn't get in to see Mr. Tyler this morning."

Sandy nodded, took the pencil from Miss Mary, and, leaning over the desk to hide what he was writing, he printed:

Dear Mr. Davis Tyler
Do you want Baltimore Colt Season Ticket on 50 Yard-line? I have 10.

                    Yours sincerely.
                    Roosevelt Tatler

After carefully sealing the envelope, he passed it on to Shipley Pine, even though Miss Mary held out her hand and said, "Don't worry, I'll handle it, Mr. Pine." As soon as the guard saw that business done, he reached out and took Sandy by the elbow. Once out of the room, he took a rougher hold, almost pushing and pulling Sandy along the corridor. "Leggo, man," Sandy protested, but this only encouraged the guard to be meaner. He made Sandy walk like a prisoner down the steps, holding him by the back of his belt, and at the bottom he refused to let him go until he had issued several warnings about what he would personally do to Sandy's private parts should he ever trouble Mr. Tyler and Miss Mary again.

At last he released his hold, and Sandy took a first quick step toward the door. But he froze in the next instant, like everyone in the bank, for from above came desperate screams and, behold, Miss Mary dashing along like a sprint man. She paused long enough at the top of the stairs to point a finger directly at Sandy and cry, "Stop him! Don't let that colored boy get away!"

Sandy's mouth flew open. The one guard who had just let

him go literally leaped on him, knocking him to the ground, and others ran to the spot with drawn pistols. The guard pulled Sandy's left arm up behind his back as he lay on the ground, forcing it higher and higher until Sandy thought it would break.

Miss Mary arrived, gasping, her tic galloping across her face, and, without admonishing the guard, said, "I'm so glad you didn't get away. Mr. Tyler read your note and would like to see you."

"Leggo," Sandy cried.

"Don't worry, Miss Mary, I'll hold the nigger till the police get here," the guard said.

"No, Harry, let him up," Miss Mary said. "Mr. Tyler wants to see him."

"Mr. Tyler does?" the guard said, a vacant look crossing his face. He let go, and Sandy sprang up, shaking his arm. He leaned down and picked up his hat, brushed it off, and, making sure that there was no further mistake, and that all the pistols had been returned to their holsters, he strode past Miss Mary, took the steps two at a time, and walked briskly down the hall to where Davis Tyler waited impatiently for him outside his office door. He shook Sandy's hand warmly and, clasping him about the far shoulder, directed him into his office and to the soft leather chair across from his desk. "I'll try to get back to you, Shipley," he told Pine just before he closed the door. Shipley Pine just shook his head in wonderment at what powers the mysterious young Negro must possess.

Miss Mary struggled back to the office, flushed and out of breath, and reached for another Hit Parade. "I'll tell you, Mr. Pine, I've never seen it to fail," she exclaimed. "Colored people just always cause trouble."

8

Splitting the Uprights

In all his short life, Sandy had never had any real negotiations
with white people. His neighborhood, his schools, and, at last,
his outlook were all necessarily black. The reason that he was
now sitting in the office of the most powerful banker in Baltimore was not, however, because Sandy perceived L. Davis Tyler
to be some great white father he had to turn to. On the con-
trary, Sandy saw him only as an associate. Sandy Tatler was,
obviously, a very bright young man. It was just that never before
had he been presented with a situation that so tested his intelli-
gence.

Sandy had concluded very quickly that he had obtained the
tickets only through some large error, and that the slightest mis-
calculation on his part would reveal that error to someone and
result in his losing the tickets. By himself he had no chance. At
first he considered throwing in his lot with Howard Winfrey,
the richest black man he knew, who ran a Betholine-Sinclair
service station down the street, but on some reflection Sandy

decided that Howard Winfrey meant no more to the white world than did Sandy Tatler. Service station or not, they were both likely to be dismissed as niggers. No, Sandy realized that he had to deal with someone white, and what really proved his shrewdness was that he realized that he must not turn to some piddling white, some little loan officer or a desk man at HFC. Sandy needed a substantial white ally—and nobody was going to take any Colt tickets away from L. Davis Tyler.

The reception that he received from Tyler was so extraordinary, however, that Sandy realized he had only dimly perceived the power of his tickets. By the time the president had finished offering Sandy cigars, mints, and ice water and showing him some of the more valuable mementos of his office, Sandy realized that he was really holding all the cards. Davis Tyler was, it seemed, *anxious* to be his angel.

So, drawing a deep breath, Sandy announced, "Sir, now, Mr. Davis Tyler, sir, I have ten Colt season tickets on the fifty-yard line, Section Ten." As soon as he said that, Sandy could see Tyler preparing to ask him where the hell he got these tickets, and since Sandy did not want to get into that, he quickly handed over the ticket-application acceptance form and kept talking as fast as he could. "Now, sir, Mr. Tyler, all I want for myself is two tickets. If you will pay for my two tickets, I will give you two tickets, and you can take the other six and sell them to the other workers in the bank." Sandy did not know about expense accounts and entertaining clients, so he could not mention that possible use for the extra tickets.

Tyler nodded and turned the ticket confirmation over in his hands. "You're the R. Tatler listed at this address?" he said.

"Yes sir. That's me."

"All right," Tyler said with a flourish. "It's a deal." Sandy couldn't believe it. "On one condition," Tyler added quickly.

"Yes sir?"

"That you will give me an option on the same deal next season."

Unfortunately, Sandy did not know what "option" meant. "I don't know," he said reflexively.

"You drive a hard bargain," Tyler replied, smiling. "I'll tell you what. Give me an option on just five of the tickets next year, then four the year after that, then three, and so on—and I'll still always pay for your two. In a few years, you'll have control of all the tickets. How's that?" Sandy began to comprehend what option was. Also, for the first time, he appreciated that he was going to get these same tickets year in and year out, perpetually. That is the way it is with season tickets.

"Yes sir." Davis Tyler stuck out his hand, and they shook on it. Then he pushed a button, and Miss Mary came bustling in. "Miss Mary," Tyler said, "have a draft drawn up for my signature for $300 payable to the Baltimore Colts. Do this right away, please." Miss Mary left in a confused bustle.

Tyler leaned back in his big chair and looked carefully over at Sandy, who was smiling proudly and fingering his pork-pie hat. This had to be the smartest colored boy he had ever met. Also, it occurred to Tyler (for he was a most forward-looking man) that within a very few years banks—which is to say, especially the First Merchants Trust—were surely going to have to hire colored people as tellers and maybe even assistant branch managers and whatnot. As fast as things were going, this was a distinct possibility. "You in school, Mr. Tatler?" Tyler asked.

"Yes sir. Dunbar."

"Hmmm. You going to college?"

Sandy had never thought seriously about college. It simply wasn't a realistic possibility. After Dunbar, he had figured on joining the United States Marine Corps and maybe learning a reliable trade, or making a career of it, if he liked it.

"Yes sir," he replied. "I want to go to college."

"Well, fine," Tyler said, "and when you graduate, you come back and see me, and I'm sure there'll be a job here in the bank for you." He paused. "Maybe even as a teller."

"Yes sir," Sandy said. This was the damnedest thing he had ever heard of. Miss Mary came back with the check, and Mr. Tyler signed it.

"Now, you take this up to the Colt offices, and if there is any trouble, you have them call me direct right here. Then you bring the tickets back to me."

"Yes sir."

"You are a pleasure to do business with, Mr. Tatler."

"You are too," Sandy said, and, realizing the deal had been concluded, he rose to leave. Shipley Pine stared in amazement at him as he departed.

Sandy picked up the tickets at the Colts office, as well as the most profuse apologies from the poor clerk who had called Mr. Tyler up for a verification of his signature, and brought Tyler's eight back to him after lunch. He was introduced, effusively, to Mr. Carl Krantam of the Federal Reserve Board and served coffee at that time, as his future as a valued employee of the First Merchants Trust was discussed in detail.

Every Sunday the Colts were at home that fall he attended the games, where Mr. Tyler introduced him to Mrs. Tyler and the other dignitaries whom the bank invited to use the extra six seats. One time several city councilmen were there, and for the Detroit game most of the Board of Estimates was on hand, including Mr. Ronald Taylor. For the San Francisco game, there were Mr. and Mrs. Tyler, six other bank presidents, Sandy, and his friend Junie Ellison, whom he had sold his extra ticket to that week. With the money that Sandy obtained from the sale of this ticket every week he bought himself a snappy new suit of clothes, two shirts with Mr. B collars, and some Mojud hose for his mother.

In February, after the season, dressed in his new clothes, Sandy got on the Number 11 bus line and traveled out to Johns Hopkins University. There, for the price of two Colt season tickets—his extra and the one that reverted back to him in the bank option deal—Sandy obtained the guarantee of entrance and scholarship (one for each). He matriculated there in the fall and, after industrious study, graduated with honors as an economics major. With introductions from Davis Tyler, he was granted interviews with most financial executives in the city, which made it possible for him to write a brilliant thesis on "Branch Banking in Baltimore," a paper of such rare insight that it helped him make Phi Beta Kappa. Also, in the course of his research he encountered Shipley Pine again. For the going price of one season ticket, Pine took Sandy on as a summer employee at Pine Brothers and Moore. Sandy was the first black so employed and took the position away from the boss's son, Kempton Moore III.

Near the end of his senior year, Sandy went down to the Fifth Regiment Armory and volunteered to the sergeant there for service in the Maryland National Guard. The sergeant, one Ansel Topper, E-6, said that the quota had, sadly, just been filled only moments before. Sandy mentioned this business about a Colt season ticket on the fifty-yard line. The week following his graduation he was on the train to Fort Knox, Kentucky, a proud member—one of the few blacks in history—of the 29th Guard Division.

While Sandy was serving his six months' active duty with distinction, Davis Tyler was dispatched in an unfortunate shooting accident near Easton, Maryland, when he was, it seems, mistaken for a low-flying canvasback duck by Mrs. Tyler. While this ended Sandy's hopes for a job with First Merchants Trust, it did give him back the rights to two more season tickets, so he wrote Shipley Pine and asked him if he might like to have another ticket. Shipley said his brother, Rogers Pine, would be delighted. Immediately upon his return from active duty, Sandy assumed a job as the first black broker ever employed by Pine Brothers and Moore.

A few months later, Sandy married Cynthia Green, the daughter of a prominent black surgeon in New York. He had met Cynthia while she was attending Goucher College in Towson. The newlyweds drove away from the church in a magnificent new Oldsmobile 88, which Sandy had obtained a few days before on a sort of permanent trade-out basis from Mickey Shadducks of Mickey Shadducks Olds. Mickey was a great Colts fan.

Shortly after Sandy and Cynthia had their first child, a son, Theodore Green Tatler, Sandy approached Sergeant Ansel Topper and informed him that he would like to apply for National Guard officer's training. Sergeant Topper said that, sadly, the last vacancy had just been filled. Sandy replied that it seemed the Colt ticket he had allotted Sergeant Topper for the past three years would no longer be available to him. A check of the records, Sergeant Topper explained, showed that one officer's candidate position had just opened up unexpectedly. Sandy graduated from the course with honors and was commissioned a second lieutenant, the second black to obtain officer status in the Maryland National Guard.

At his first summer camp as an officer, at Camp A.P. Hill, Virginia, Sandy encountered Pfc Jerry Start, who was serving, disgruntled, as his platoon's pots-and-pans man on KP. Sandy discovered grease on one particularly vital pot that Jerry had allegedly cleaned, and, in true officer fashion, he explained to Jerry that this greasy pot would surely bring the whole regiment down with the worst case of diarrhea known in medical annals. Jerry, who did not like being lectured to by a black man, protested that he was miscast for this low-life assignment, he being a man of substance and stature. Jerry pointed out that he was a homeowner, about to leave one house, in Far Lake Estates, for another, finer one in Ruxton, and about to take up employment with the fine old Baltimore stock firm of Pine Brothers and Moore. Jerry dropped the pot on his foot when Sandy casually replied that he already worked for that very establishment. Not long after, for the price of one Colt season ticket (and absolution from KP), Jerry agreed to sell the house in Far Lake Estates to Lieutenant Tatler.

Thus it was that Colt season tickets had provided Sandy with an introduction to the white Establishment, with a free college education, a Phi Beta Kappa key, an escape from the draft, a National Guard commission, a fancy new-model automobile every year, a respectable white-collar job, and a neat, nice house in an otherwise all-white community. At Colt games, there on the fifty-yard line in Section 10, Sandy sat on the aisle. Next to him sat Shipley Pine, and next to him, Rogers Pine. Then came the two gentlemen from Johns Hopkins, Dean of Admissions Elton Webber and Professor T.J. Trombley of the scholarship board. Then came Sergeant Ansel Topper, Mickey Shadducks of Mickey Shadducks Olds, and Jerry Start. The two tickets at the end were provided by Sandy to exceptional, or potential, business clients. With the enticement of a fifty-yard-line ticket, Sandy was able to draw customers away from some of the most successful brokers in the city and to establish himself as a leader in the profession.

Of course, he gave these last two tickets away only on a game-to-game basis. They were Sandy's hole cards, and the other members of his season-ticket club—having learned from each other during half-time discussions how Sandy had used each of them—used to speculate on who would get those final two tickets. What more did Sandy Tatler want? Did he hope to be the first black to win membership in the Elkridge Club? A better house, maybe even in Guilford or Ruxton? Did he want to be an Episcopalian? Junior League for Cynthia? Calvert School for Theodore? A summer place on Gibson Island? Or had Sandy decided that what he really wanted was to be mayor of the whole city of Baltimore?

This was not so far-fetched as it might seem. Lesser men than Sandy, and for much less than two tickets on the fifty-yard line, had become mayors of Baltimore. Besides, thanks to a fortunate accident, Sandy had been blessed with some impressive credentials. He had become commanding officer in charge of a whole damn battalion in the Maryland National Guard. It had all happened just this summer past.

Because he was the only black officer in the Guard, none of the officers, and precious few of the NCOs either (Sergeant Ansel Topper being a notable exception), would associate with Sandy. Thus it was that one night during summer training camp at Camp A.P. Hill, Virginia, virtually every officer in the whole division except Sandy was huddled in a group watching pornographic movies, when Specialist Fourth Class Petey Riddle took a wrong turn in his vehicle. The wrong turn brought Specialist Fourth Class Riddle bearing down on the theater where all the officers were watching the skin flicks.

There were two especially unfortunate things about the incident. One was that the theater was outside, an open-air site. The other unfortunate thing was that the vehicle that Specialist Fourth Class Riddle was driving was an M-49 Sherman tank.

Specialist Fourth Class Riddle was, nominally, a clerk-typist, but there was an IG inspection coming up, and the Guard did not have enough tank-drivers, so he was pressed into service as a driver so that the division could pass inspection with an "Excellent" rating. Sadly, once he squashed, in whole or in part, 263 officers, the division was marked off in the category of "vehicular organization and planning" and thus was granted only a "Superior" inspection rating. Also, a leadership vacuum was created.

In a panic, the Guard put a computer to work to determine what survivor should take over the Baltimore battalion. Because the only remaining officers that outranked First Lieutenant Tatler were chaplains, the computer determined that Sandy should be jumped to colonel and given full command of the battalion. Thus did Sandy Tatler become the only black commanding officer in two hundred years of the National Guard, with the exception of Enos Tyrell, who headed the Mississippi Guard for a brief period in 1867. Sandy was promptly placed on the boards of three hospitals, two schools, a museum, a poverty program, and an educational TV station.

With the new title and authority, and the two extra season tickets, there appeared to be no way that Sandy could fail to reach the mayoralty. In fact, there was only one thing that could mar this path, a fateful event that had occurred only a few days before Specialist Fourth Class Riddle's tank and the computer had elevated Sandy to high command.

Being a devoted Colt fan, Sandy had been a charter member of what was then called the Afro-American Colt Stampede. The A-ACS—originally the NCS, the Negro Colt Stampede; later the BCS, the Black Colt Stampede; and most recently the CSS, the Colt Soul Stampede—met every Monday for lunch at the Elite Club on Pennsylvania Avenue and included in its membership some of the most influential black people in the city. Naturally, Sandy had become president.

Following the August 16 luncheon, devoted primarily to slow-motion films of the Atlanta exhibition game that had been played a few days earlier in Lubbock, Texas, Third Vice-President Henry Carroll asked Sandy to stay afterward for some crucial A-ACS executive business. As soon as all the other members had departed, however, Carroll pulled back a rug and opened a secret trapdoor. A young man jumped out, and, even with his disguise, Sandy realized instantly who he was. He was Tyrone Dancer, on the lam.

Henry Carroll laid it on the line. Tyrone Dancer was to go home with Tatler and hide in his house until a way could be found to spirit him out of the country. Surely, Carroll explained, Dancer would be safe at the Tatlers', for no one would ever think of looking for the man who put LSD in all the National Guard canteens in the very house of a National Guard officer.

Sandy understood that there was no way in which he could decline to take on Dancer. If he refused, the word would soon be out that he was a sell-out to his race. Besides, Sandy liked what he knew of Dancer and approved of much that he had done. So he embraced him warmly and drove him home, listening to all the broadcasts declaring that the black sections of all Eastern metropolitan cities were under tight surveillance. Nobody, of course, was watching Far Lake Estates, where Tyrone Dancer was soon comfortably sequestered in the guest room of the Roosevelt Tatler home.

Three days later Sandy departed for summer camp. In another two weeks, after Specialist Fourth Class Riddle had run amok, Dancer was not only the guest of a Guardsman but a guest of the only black commander in the whole country. Or, for most of the day, he was the guest of the wife of the only black commander. It was not his career that Sandy fretted for. It was his marriage. Day after day, his wife was alone in his house, alone with a small child and with the most dynamic, persuasive, and charismatic leader in the United States.

Even if it took his last two Colt season tickets, Sandy decided that he had to get Tyrone Dancer out of his house, out of Far Lake Estates, out of Baltimore, and out of the country.

9

Bump-and-Run

Whereas Sandy, with his season tickets, had become a political power to be reckoned with, Jerry had made more of a name for himself in the financial community. This was largely on account of Fewster C.P. Benton IV, socialite and holder of much of the most valuable land in the Green Spring Valley, where all the best families and horses in Baltimore lived. Fewster C.P. Benton IV was the son of Fewster C.P. Benton III. Because Fewster was such a horrible name, everybody had always called the elder Benton "Skippy," and they continued to, even as he aged gracelessly into alcoholism. Nonetheless, much as Fewster III hated the name of Fewster, the first shot he got, he named his son after himself. Then they immediately started calling the poor kid "Young Skippy." The Bentons also had a daughter, Agnes, who was named for her mother, and although she grew to five feet, eleven and a half inches, towering over her mother from the age of twelve, she was always known as "Little Agnes."

Two of the saddest, most mixed-up kids you ever saw growing up in your life were Young Skippy and Little Agnes. Neither fully recovered, although Little Agnes did learn to be well received in some circles when she took up nymphomania as a hobby. Never so clever as his sister, Young Skippy just drifted into the humdrum life of a Colts fan. He was so boring about the Colts that he could actually bore other Colt fans. Of course, Jerry figured that you could never be sure when Young Skippy might want to switch brokers, so he made himself talk to Young Skippy about outside linebackers at the Colt Stampede luncheons.

The morning after Jerry had struggled through one Stampede session with Young Skippy, Kempton Moore, a partner at Pine Brothers and Moore, invited Jerry to come duck-hunting with him that weekend. The Colts were playing Chicago at home that Sunday, but Jerry could not possibly turn down an invitation from the boss, and he accepted precipitously. This left Jerry with his fifty-yard-line ticket, so he took a page from Sandy's book and decided to use it as a business advantage. He called up Young Skippy and offered him the seat.

Young Skippy, whose own seat was in the temporary end-zone structure, was ecstatic at this windfall and grew even more profusely thankful when the Colts won 56–7, with Johnny Unitas throwing four touchdown passes and setting several impressive records. Young Skippy assured Jerry that his great generosity would someday be repaid, and sure enough, a few months later Young Skippy called up and said he could get Jerry in on the ground floor of a new concept in franchising. What exactly he said was, "Jerry, I can get you in on the ground floor of a new concept in franchising."

Jerry grew especially intrigued because Young Skippy actually wanted Jerry to meet the president of the franchise operation at lunch. Jerry had never met a company president before, except for Shipley Pine, but of course he was the president of his own company, so that really did not count. That Young Skippy's president turned out at lunch to be twenty-four years old with some baby fat, residual adolescent acne, and a clip-on bow tie did not diminish his presidential presence any. After all, Jerry's dear old friend and confidant, Young Skippy Benton, was to be executive vice-president. Their joint acumen became manifest when the two men informed Jerry that they wanted him to sell the new company's initial stock offering.

Jerry shifted all these facts and arrived at a decision. This is a can't-miss proposition, he thought. Not only that, but Jerry liked what the new company was up to. He said that it sounded like a good business idea, even if there was not a stock market to put it in. What the new company planned to do was to franchise quick-clip barbershops, locating them in the spare corners of hamburger stands that had previously been reserved for mustard dispensers and waste receptacles. According to Young Skippy, a man could get a good haircut in the time that it took to prepare and salt an order of french-fries. A customer could get a trim and a shampoo while waiting for a double-decked hamburger and a milkshake to be prepared. The barbershops were going to operate under the name of Cut 'N' Run.

Enthralled at the prospects, Jerry immediately agreed to handle the sale of $400,000 worth of stock, with shares priced at $10. First, he sold everything he owned in the market, and, working heavily on margin, bought the first $80,000 himself. With little effort, he unloaded the rest on his best customers. Everybody was anxious to get in on the ground floor of a can't-miss proposition. Nor was it long, either, before Jerry's sagacity was proved. Cut 'N' Run doubled to 20 in the first hour that it was traded, and closed the day at 47⅜ bid, over the counter. Then it really took off.

Jerry would occasionally acknowledge that Cut 'N' Run had been issued at a felicitous boom time, but nonetheless even he, in all modesty, could not deny that it was truly a super stock.

In fact, the day it passed 100, Jerry said to Rosalie, "Would you believe SuperStock?" He had calculated once, and then explained to her, that their lifetime prosperity was assured for so long as the Dow Jones averages dipped no lower than 800, or, possibly, to the 770 support level, whatever that was. This extremely unlikely possibility provided much comfort to the Starts on those rare so-called Blue Mondays when the market was buffeted by technical adjustments.

But Cut 'N' Run soon removed all financial worries. Jerry had so much of C 'N' R stock that he was moved to put some in Rosalie's and the children's names, and the way it continued going up, Jerry soon calculated that Rosalie and the two kids were "rich in their own right." In fact, everybody who had bought the stock from Jerry, which was just about everybody who knew and trusted his judgment, had become filthy rich.

Of course, only truly sage market analysts could have perceived the long-term bonanza. When Cut 'N' Run first offered the sale of stock, the prospectus indicated that there were present plans calling for only one actual barbershop, that in a rundown fried-chicken emporium in Seaford, Delaware. Nonetheless, within a short period the stock was moving at 220. This was only 95 times earnings, however, so naturally the company took the opportunity to expand and diversify. With the overwhelming consent of the confident stockholders, Cut 'N' Run purchased a poorly managed research firm, Wonder Associates of Timonium, Maryland.

After this acquisition, C 'N' R stock rose modestly to 255, and Jerry was hailed in the profession as a legend in his own time. Even Sandy Tatler, although eaten up by jealousy, had put everything he and Cynthia owned into C 'N' R when it hit 60—and all his customers' money too. As Jerry soon found out, however, money can be merely listless and dull as dishwater when it just sits there. Certainly neither he nor any of his clients wanted to unload just yet; they were all waiting for C 'N' R to sprint up another couple of hundred points or so, and then they could get out at the top with a real killing. As a consequence, Jerry had nothing much to occupy him, especially during the Colts' off-season, and so he just lolled around the office, idly watching the up-ticks on the market tape and peering down fronts. One day, as he grew bored musing on a possible schedule of events for him and Mary Ellen Doherty in Municipal Bonds, should they ever be stranded together overnight in the same Holiday Inn room somewhere, Jerry decided to drive out to the laboratories of Wonder Associates, the Cut 'N' Run subsidiary.

A fellow in a long white smock, who was the chief engineer, greeted Jerry, and when Jerry advised him of his substantial interest in the firm, the engineer invited him to inspect the main Wonder project. He led Jerry into a huge room, which was piled high with stacks of some strange green material. "Thar she blows," said the engineer.

"What is it?" Jerry asked.

"What's it look like?" the head engineer said.

"Well," Jerry replied, "it just sort of looks like a lot of green stuff to me."

"You're right as far as you go," the head engineer said.

"But it's got to be trickier than that."

The engineer lowered his voice. "Mr. Start," he said, "you bet it is. You are looking at the world's newest technological breakthrough, Bingo Turf."

Jerry nodded, and then he remembered to say, "What is Bingo Turf?"

The engineer, whose name was Andy, just smiled and led Jerry over to the stacks. "Go on," he said. Jerry ran his fingers all through it. "Well, what's it feel like?"

Jerry said, "Well, it's kind of hard to say. It's kind of like a piece of sandy pussy at the beach."

Andy wrinkled his nose somewhat. "I've never quite heard it described that way before."

"No, you couldn't use it in the advertising," Jerry said.

"No, you couldn't."

"Well, what is Bingo Turf?" Jerry asked again.

"Mr. Start," Andy said, "Bingo Turf is an effort to create an artificial grass that will be within the means of the average middle-class American family."

"You mean anybody can afford this, instead of a lawn or real grass?" Jerry cried.

"You better believe it," Andy said, smiling broadly, and patting a stack for emphasis. "This stuff can be what television sets were a generation ago, or sliced bread a generation before that."

"Jesus," Jerry said, "how did Cut 'N' Run get into a thing like this?"

"Originally," the head engineer said, "this was going to be a revolutionary new kind of toupee."

"Bingo Turf was?"

"Well, it wasn't called Bingo Turf then, as a toupee."

"What was it called?"

"When it started out as a toupee, it was called Rug-A-Dug-Dug. We could never work it out, though, Rug-A-Dug-Dug, so that's when we switched it around and made it green and went for the Bingo Turf angle."

"Why aren't we mass-producing this stuff?" Jerry shrieked. He was getting excited. "This could be a bonanza. We got to get this stuff out to a mass consumer market."

"That's the trouble," the head engineer said.

"What trouble?"

"Getting it down to a price that is compatible to a mass market. Our projections are that Bingo Turf could take off if we could sell the thing at $1.06 a square foot. We couldn't sell the stuff fast enough at that price. Unfortunately, if we got all the bugs out of it, we figure it would cost us so much that we would have to sell it at $860 a square foot, give or take a few cents, to make a profit."

"That's a big difference," Jerry acknowledged.

"Yes it is, but if we can just iron out the imperfections, this sonofabitch will sell like hot cakes. At $1.06 a square foot, every John Doe in America would have to buy Bingo Turf. I mean, he would have to."

Jerry left in a glorious daze. The existence of Bingo Turf and its potential overwhelmed him, and the thought of being the first man in his neighborhood, even in all of suburban Baltimore, to have his lawn fitted entirely with artificial grass became an obsession with him. Finally he went out to the laboratory and prevailed upon Andy to give him an eight-foot by ten-foot slice of Bingo Turf that was a factory reject.

Of course, to this point, all Bingo Turf was factory reject. That was the trouble. Nonetheless, Jerry first tried to convince Rosalie to employ the specimen as a living-room rug. Failing that (because the Bingo Turf clashed with the decorator furnishings), Jerry convinced Rosalie to feature it as a scatter rug in the children's playroom. Unfortunately, this led to the discovery of one of the imperfections in the product, for it turned out that if anybody put any weight on the Bingo Turf, the little green fibers pulled out and embedded themselves in the skin. Halfback, the schnauzer, had to be taken to the veterinarian's to have the sharp little green particles removed following his first casual encounter with the surface. So Jerry had no recourse but to exile his beloved piece of Bingo Turf to the utility room, next to his club cellar, where the washer and drier were kept.

Publicly, however, Bingo Turf thrived on rumors that its little quirks were about to be ironed out. Jerry got Sandy Tatler to use part of his battalion commander's office in the Fifth Regiment Armory as a sort of downtown showcase for Bingo Turf. They piled up a huge stack of the stuff there and took prospective stock purchasers over to look at it and caress it. The good reports about Bingo Turf's progress helped to drive up the

C 'N' R stock some more, and it really soared again when an announcement was made that Cut 'N' Run was actually going to open a second barbershop, this one in a bar-B-Q establishment on the outskirts of Oil City, Pennsylvania.

The stock had carried so high that even Jerry was brushed by a zephyr of caution. He called up Rosalie one day and told her to unload one hundred shares of the C 'N' R that he had given her and the kids. "But don't you think it will go higher?" Rosalie asked, just as all people asked brokers in those days.

"Well, New York says it's wise to take a firmer cash position," Jerry replied. "That will put more than twenty thousand in your savings account, even after capital gains. You know what they say along Wall Street: bulls can win and bears can win, but pigs never do."

Rosalie agreed to sell the one hundred shares quietly to the broker husband of an old Sweet Briar college roommate of hers in Richmond; in fact, she was secretly delighted with the transaction. While Rosalie would never admit this to herself, she feared sometimes that Jerry really was not a certified financial wizard. It was not only that he had departed the University of Maryland in haste before he could be flunked out. His arithmetic was invariably faulty, and although he protested that Einstein had failed a test in this subject in school, Rosalie was not altogether satisfied that the rebuttal was germane. Also, try as she might, she simply could not believe that punts, first downs, and fumble-recoveries could truly be the keys to the stock market. For that matter, she could not comprehend, either, why Cut 'N' Run should be the top performance stock in all the land.

Of course, as Jerry often reminded her, "The big thing we really got going for us is that haircuts are one thing that are never out of style."

10

Double Coverage

While Jerry had become established as a most successful broker even before he landed in Cut 'N' Run, Rosalie also knew that he had been required to depend almost entirely on the Colts and the mad pro football environment in Baltimore to achieve any progress in his profession.

When Jerry had first started selling stocks he could not find any customers, besides Reds Ritchie, outside of his immediate family. There was no reason for anyone to shift his business to Jerry inasmuch as, during these years, every stock went up, no matter who the broker was. Jerry sent out letters and made telephone calls and pounded the streets for months without even limited success. He had made a lot of money in the market for himself, but had converted all that into a down payment on the fancy new house in Ruxton. His commissions could not keep up the mortgage; and besides, the second child was on the way. Jerry grew depressed and irritable. He had to start making more money, and soon.

This disconsolate time happened to fall just before the start of the 1964 pro football season. As a matter of fact, Jerry grew so discouraged on the Friday afternoon before the Colts' opening game with Minnesota that he gave up trying to scare up any new business and just turned into the first bar he came across. He ordered a double bourbon on the rocks. Not surprisingly, the bar talk was concerned exclusively with pro football, and most especially with the Colts' opener. Minnesota was a weak expansion club, though, so the only speculation revolved around how much the Colts would win by. Jerry, feeling sorrier and meaner with each drink, decided to help make everyone's life as sour as his own.

"Minnesota will kick the living shit out of the Colts," he announced loudly and profanely. Immediately the whole bar fell deadly silent, with only embarrassed coughs and the shaking of ice cubes—cough, cough, tinkle, cough, tinkle, tinkle, cough, and so on. Jerry kept going. "Look, the Colts are overconfident. Tarkenton will start scrambling around, and in the heat out there, the Colts' front four will feel about a hundred years old by half time."

The other patrons and the bartender just stared at Jerry. Most of them were in shock. Finally a bald-headed hardware salesman named Neil pulled himself together and delivered his measured judgment: "You're full of shit, buddy." With that, everybody else breathed the air out and started shuffling feet and making grumbling noises. Jerry, however, was growing stronger in his drink and his anonymity, and started talking about charts and figures and contacts and his own expert analyses, all of which indicated conclusively that Minnesota would upset the Colts. At last he was required to make a few small bets (begging off any large amounts by maintaining that he had no desire to rob these uninformed unfortunates, only teach them a lesson), and he left his money with the bartender. Then Jerry went home and forgot the whole episode until Sunday, when he was utterly stunned to watch as Minnesota really did upset the Colts, 34-20.

Since he had $8 coming to him from the bets he had covered, Jerry returned to the bar, which was called the New Italy Pub and Grill. He only wanted to pick up his money, but he found himself greeted as an honored celebrity. Many of the same people had been in attendance the Friday before, and they introduced him to newcomers as a seer and expert both. Everyone solicited his opinion of the next game, against Green Bay, but Jerry, who just wanted to get his $8 and clear out of the place, begged off modestly, apologizing that he had not yet completed his research for this game. "Besides," he explained, "I don't pretend to be able to pick all the games. There's only a few, like last week, when I'm absolutely positive."

Everybody clustered about him and begged him to come back whenever he had another sure winner, and a little round man named Herb said, "Hey Jer, what do you do, anyways?"

"You mean like for a living?" Jerry asked.

"Yeah, your job, like."

"I'm a stockbroker."

Herb asked, "Yeah? D'you know the market like you know the Colts?"

Jerry chuckled suavely like Cesar Romero himself and said, "What d'you think, Baby Cakes? The Colts are a hobby; the market's my game."

Herb said, "Judas Priest, would I like to have a guy like you handlin' my stuff." The words burst into Jerry's brain and, like a dum-dum bullet, exploded all over the place. He looked down at Herb and all the others, who were staring back up at him with blind trust, saying things like, "That's for sure now," and, "Don't you just know it," and, "A license to print money." Jerry sized them up in a hurry: they were all nickel-dime odd-lotters, a $25-war-bond crowd. Jerry bought a round for the house and then hustled out of the New Italy Pub and Grill as fast as he could. His mind was racing.

Within a few hours Jerry had the whole scheme worked out, and all the next week he cased bars throughout the metropolitan area, from Glen Burnie south to Catonsville west, to Timonium north and around to Middle River east. He must have gone into a hundred places, limiting himself to a beer in each, which he drank slowly and unobtrusively, as he studied the clientele and the ambience. By his calculations, Jerry figured that he needed sixteen bars to start with. They had to be located far apart; they had to be first-class establishments with wealthy patrons who were devoted to the Colts but who did not know Jerry. One slip-up, and the whole jig was up.

It took him nearly two weeks before he settled on his sixteen bars, a period in which Rosalie grew madder by the night. All she knew was that every night he came home late and half in the bag. Besides, with all his time spent auditioning bars, Jerry's commissions had dropped to $71.46 one week and $54.20 the next, so Rosalie had been forced to start dipping into their slim savings account to pay the mortgage and the car installments. She warned him that unless his business picked up they would be dead broke around the first of the year.

"Don't you understand, Jerry?" Rosalie cried. "We won't even have enough money to afford a hospital for the baby. We'll be the first people in Ruxton ever to have a midwife."

In response, he tried to coo and kiss her, but she backed away and literally held him at arm's length. "Goddamn it, Rosalie," Jerry said. "This is one time you got to take me on faith—"

"Don't give me that one-time stuff, Jerry. I married you on faith and before that I let you inside my pants on faith—"

"Rosalie, for God's sake!"

"I just wanted to bring the on-faith scoreboard up to date."

"All right, I'm telling you for the last time," Jerry whined. "I'm not chasing any broads, I'm not drinking nearly as much as you think I am, and I'm not doing anything illegal."

"Well, if you're not doing any of those, you might just as well stay home," Rosalie said.

"I promise you, I'll explain it all when it's over," Jerry cried, grabbing for her.

"I promise you, it'll all be over by the time you explain," Rosalie called back, and she stomped up the stairs, stopping only long enough to point down at him and add, "And keep your sticky whisky fingers off my radiant fertile body."

The next week Jerry began his scheme in earnest. The Colts had not lost since the opener against Minnesota, and their opponent, St. Louis, was undefeated. The time was ripe. The whole town was heated up about the game, and Jerry had his work cut out for him. He had sixteen bars to hit, so he had to start the caper Wednesday night. He would have opened Tuesday, but that was National Guard night.

He began at the Tally-Ho Tavern, off the beltway over in Essex. He seated himself there at the bar and began to talk football in a loud voice. He made it plain that he was a student of the game, with access to inside information, and with a secret formula that could reveal winners. He declared that his figures proved conclusively that the Colts would beat St. Louis. There was no doubt, he said, and he was never wrong.

Some of the customers found him a bit noisy and officious, but since Jerry was, after all, touting a Baltimore victory, nobody got too upset with him. He departed the Tally-Ho after a couple of hours and cut across town to the Pimlico area and Sid's 209 Club, where he pulled off the same act as he had at the Tally-Ho. Next he worked the same routine at the Dew-Drop Inn in Pikesville, and finished up with an identical performance downtown at Chaucer's. In each place he boasted often and loudly about his knowledge of pro football, with an unequivocal declaration that the Colts would beat St. Louis.

Thursday night he hit four more spots with an exact duplication of his Wednesday night act.

Friday night he also worked four more bars, and he repeated his performance in every detail except one. In these four places Jerry said that his special figures proved that St. Louis would win. Saturday he visited four more gin mills, making four more smug predictions that St. Louis would win. He did not reach home until well after two Sunday morning, because in the bars where he touted St. Louis people had a mind to argue with him, and even to try to punch him. He found a note from Rosalie telling him not to soil her bed with his presence. He slept on the sofa.

The Colts beat St. Louis easily, 47–27. Jerry took a heavy pencil and crossed a line through the names of the eight bars that he had visited Friday and Saturday nights, the ones where he had said St. Louis would win. He has not been back to any of those places since.

The next Wednesday, Jerry started hitting the other eight bars again. In each place he would start off by saying, "Well, I gave you the winner." This did not carry much weight, as the Colts were always just about everybody's choice, but Jerry added to his credence by showing a new, more dignified face. He was quieter, politer, and refused to offer an opinion on the upcoming game, saying, "I only talk when my figures prove that it's a sure thing." This impressed people, and Jerry led them on by visiting the same eight bars the next week, but again refusing to make any predictions. By now the regulars in most of the bars were begging Jerry to let them in on the next good thing he came up with.

Jerry made $62.49 in commissions that week, most of which went in the bars. The savings account dwindled lower. The one time Rosalie talked to him, she warned him that they would have to put the house on the market January 1. "We'll be okay by then," Jerry said, but he told her no more. This was a big week coming up.

The Colts were heavily favored over the Detroit Lions. Jerry made up his schedule of appointments. On Wednesday, he visited the Tally-Ho and Kitty Simpson's Rebel Room. There was no doubt, he boldly informed the patrons of both: the Colts were a cinch to win. Thursday he drank at the Proud Feather and the Plantation Room, where he also revealed that Baltimore would win. Friday, Jerry dropped by Chaucer's and the Dew-Drop Inn. There was no question about it, he declared in both places: the Lions would upset. On Saturday, he had the same shocking news for customers at Sid's 209 Club and the Royal Crabhouse.

Detroit walloped the Colts 31–14. Jerry took out his pencil and crossed off the four bars he had visited Wednesday and Thursday, the ones where he had predicted a Colts victory. He has never returned to any of them.

When he began putting in appearances at the other four saloons, however, he was greeted as a celebrity. Jerry Start, alone in the city of Baltimore, perhaps in the whole country, had positively guaranteed a great upset. He was never permitted to pick up a check. In fact, at Chaucer's, Mike the bartender told Jerry that everything was on the house because he was attracting business. People were bringing their friends around to meet this man who could tell the winners in advance. Jerry was never permitted to leave any one of his four remaining bars until the two a.m. closing time.

By now, Rosalie communicated with him only through the medium of notes. She wrote that they had been forced to cut out on orange juice, had to switch from English muffins to regular bread, and from premium to regular gas. Jerry's commissions dropped to $33.18.

Late in November, Jerry decided that it was time for another prediction. His fans were getting itchy. At Sid's 209 Club and the Dew-Drop Inn, he gave out the bad news—"I hate to do this, but"—that San Francisco would beat the Colts. Gloom covered these places with this revelation, and they were both quickly emptied as the patrons went home to contemplate in private the sadness of an upcoming Colt defeat. It was like New Year's Eve at Chaucer's and the Royal Crabhouse, however, when Jerry stood up to declare that his figures showed conclusively that the Colts would whip the Forty-Niners.

Baltimore won 14–3.

They waited in anger for Jerry's return to Sid's 209 and the Dew-Drop Inn. Luckily, Jerry had never provided his correct last name, because Curly, one particularly distraught Dew-Drop regular, wanted to find Jerry's house and burn it down, and/or castrate him. Many vigilantes at the bar volunteered enthusiastically for either of these projects. But, of course, they never saw Jerry again.

At the Royal Crabhouse, on the other hand, everyone whooped and hollered and sang "For He's a Jolly Good Fellow" when Jerry entered, and at Chaucer's a young man in a wheelchair was brought over to shake Jerry's hand, on the chance that his powers might be curative as well as prophetic. Three different women propositioned him, one exposing her left breast in the process, and everyone vied for the honor of buying him drinks. In each place, crowds formed five and six deep about Jerry, all struggling to hear his comments about pro football.

The Colts themselves rolled on to the championship of the Western Division, undefeated since the Detroit upset that Jerry had called. Everyone solicited Jerry for his predictions about the last two regular-season games, but he refused to offer a selection. "My figures are not quite revealing enough," he declared. "And you know, I never talk unless I'm sure. Unless *I know*. I just don't blow smoke."

At Chaucer's, a large man named Carter Wakefield, who was

the most successful insurance general agent in town, said, "We know you're always right, Jerry."

"If I get some conclusive computations on the championship game, you guys in here will be the first to know," Jerry said.

Carter Wakefield said, "God bless you."

The championship game of the National Football League was then—in the days before the Super Bowl—a meeting between the two divisional winners. This particular year, 1964, the Colts and the Cleveland Browns were the championship opponents, with Baltimore a huge favorite. A week before the game, Jerry informed his constituency at his two remaining bars that he felt that he might be able to reveal to them the winner later in the week. An unbearable suspense began to build.

On Wednesday he flipped a coin. It came up heads, so he drove down to Glen Burnie and told a hushed crowd at the Royal Crabhouse that the Colts would indeed win. Cheers rent the air, Jerry was lifted on the shoulders of some of the heartier drinkers and carried about the room, as men and women alike cried and embraced each other. There was revelry throughout the long night.

Thursday was Christmas Eve, which Jerry agreed to devote to his family. For the sake of the impressionable young Jerry Jr., Rosalie once again talked to her husband as they decorated the tree. They had been unable to buy presents for each other, and there was only canned food left in the house, save for one package of Esskay frankfurters. The heat and phone bills were long overdue, and Rosalie had to purchase New York State wine instead of imported Lancers. There was just enough in the savings account to handle one more car payment. She had already quietly started looking for another small row house back in Far Lake Estates.

Right after he put the angel on the top of the tree, Jerry reached for his overcoat and said, "I got to go out for a while."

"For God's sake honey, it's Christmas Eve," Rosalie said, and for the first time since all this started, she really began to cry a little. There were Christmas carols coming from the stereo, and Halfback wore a big red ribbon around his neck. "At least, Christmas," Rosalie said. Big tears rolled down her face.

"I know what day it is," Jerry said, looking away from her. "Look, Baby Cakes, some people have to work Christmas, whether they like it or not. Washington crossed the Delaware on Christmas. Firemen and disk jockeys and lots of guys have to work Christmas."

"What are you up to, Jerry?" Rosalie cried as he moved to the door. "Please, what is it?"

"I'll tell you next week. I've only got to do this one more time." And he leaned over and kissed his wife on the forehead. "I'll be back to put the toys out."

At Chaucer's, Jerry affected a long face, so that even before he supplied the incredible news that the Colts would lose, the people there could sense defeat. They listened quietly. "I'm sorry to have to be the one to tell you this," Jerry said, standing on a chair, "but my figures are never wrong, and they say that the Browns will win Sunday."

"Merry fucking Christmas," Mike the bartender said, and others began to sob softly.

Carter Wakefield grabbed Jerry by the shoulders and hugged him. "Don't blame yourself, boy," he said. "It's not your fault that you're the only one in the whole country who really knows the game of pro football." Heads bowed, the people filed out of Chaucer's. Mike put away the decorations that he had bought on the assumption that Jerry would announce that the Colts would win. He called up and canceled the band. Jerry shook Mike's hands and said good night, though Jerry knew that it was also good-by, because he would never be able to come back to Chaucer's after his Colts beat the stuffings out of Cleveland.

Jerry knew as well as the next fellow that the Browns did not belong on the same field as the Colts.

Two days later the Browns shut out the Colts 27–0 in the most incredible upset in the entire history of professional football.

Apparently the only people in Baltimore who were prepared for this result—and who had, in fact, bet on the Browns—were the people who hung out at Chaucer's. They all got rich. Besides, more important, none of them suffered the depression and mental anguish that befell the rest of the population.

Jerry himself was so upset by the Colts' loss that it was Wednesday before he could even work up the desire to return to Chaucer's. Then he called up Reds Ritchie and filled him in on the whole scheme. Reds departed for Chaucer's at 5 o'clock. At 5:10 he casually said to Mike the bartender, "Hey, what time is it? I'm supposed to meet Jerry here at five-thirty."

"Jerry's coming in today?" Mike cried.

"He told me to meet him here at five-thirty," Reds said. "We've got some business to discuss."

"Hey, Jerry's coming at five-thirty," Mike yelled, and everybody cheered and ran for the telephones to call their friends. Mike called down for more beer on ice, and three extra waitresses were pulled off the dining room and into the bar. Within minutes the place began to fill up.

"Yes sir," Reds said again. "I've got some business to discuss with Jerry."

"Business?" said Mike. "What kind of business."

"Well, you know, the stock market," Reds said. "Jerry is a stockbroker."

"He never said that," Mike said. "Hey, listen to this, Jerry's a stockbroker," he cried, and the people began to gather around Reds.

"Well, sure," Reds said. "You people never heard of Jerry

Start, the stockbroker? He's the best in the business. He's never wrong."

"Judas Priest," Carter Wakefield said. "Does he pick stocks like he picks football games?"

"Hell," Reds said. "You bet he does. Football is his hobby, but the market's his game."

Murmur noises swept the room. People crushed forward to hear Reds talk about where the pro football sage was employed and how he had a sixth sense for picking profitable stocks. Eighteen different people bought Reds drinks. By 5:35, when Jerry arrived, Chaucer's was literally packed with humans. Mike had to climb up on the bar and order a path made for Jerry. He moved through it, nodding this way and that, as if he were blessing the assembled.

At the bar Jerry picked up one of the fourteen bourbon-and-waters still lined up in front of Reds and smiled benignly at his friends. He raised his glass and spoke. "A toast to our beloved Colts. Our team in victory or defeat."

"Hooray, hooray," the people called, raising their glasses.

Jerry turned back, and the crowds began to press to him. Carter Wakefield, wheezing at Reds' elbow, could not contain himself any longer. "I didn't know you were a stockbroker, Jerry," he said.

"No, I didn't know that," Mike added.

"No, no, we didn't know," many of the people said.

"Ahh, you know, I never like to talk business at the bar," Jerry said.

"Well, then, could I come by your office tomorrow?" Wakefield asked. "I've got a brokerage account in six figures, and I'd like you to handle it."

"Oh, sure," Jerry said. "Here's my card. You can never have too much business."

"Can I have one too?" asked Mike, and Jerry gave him a card.

"Me too, me too," the people cried, jamming forward to receive cards. They came at him in waves. The next day, at Pine Brothers and Moore, Jerry made more sales than the entire firm had in the combined months of July and August and the first two weeks in September. At one point the line of prospective customers, many of them grasping cash, stretched out through the lobby and onto Redwood Street, even though the thermometer stood at 18 degrees. There were so many customers waiting to see Jerry that Pine Brothers and Moore had to send over to the Century Theatre for ushers and ropes and stanchions to control the crowd. In commissions that day alone, Jerry made $47,627 and change. The next day another $32,863 in commissions dribbled in. After the market closed, he sent checks over to the bank to buy his car and house outright; he bought a full-length mink coat for Rosalie and called her up and told her to meet him at the Chesapeake Restaurant at 6:30 sharp. She said she didn't have enough money to pay for a babysitter, let alone for a meal at the Chesapeake. Jerry said, "Be there, Baby Cakes."

The Chesapeake rented him a whole room and a violinist. After the shrimp cocktail and the first bottle of wine, Jerry pulled out the mortgage and the car loan, tore them to shreds, and let the pieces fall all over the place. Then at last he explained to Rosalie what exactly he had been up to all these months. When they left and stopped to pick up their coats, the claim-check girl gave Rosalie the full-length mink. Jerry told the girl to keep the coat Rosalie had worn in as a tip. And he gave her a five for her trouble, too.

Rosalie rode home snuggled next to Jerry. He told her just to leave her old Falcon station wagon in the lot. The people from Towson Ford could pick it up when they brought the Country Squire the next day. They climbed into bed together as soon as they got home, mad with love for each other, even if Rosalie was going on seven months' pregnant and embarrassed about her girth. After smothering him with kisses, nibbling on his ear, and so on and so forth, Rosalie grabbed him passionately and cried, "I knew you were smart, Jerry, but I never knew I married a genius."

Jerry pulled her to him and whispered, "You never know how you look till you get your picture took."

11

Naked Reverse

Baltimore had never seen anything like it when Toby showed up Tuesday for his first practice with the Colts at Memorial Stadium. The national press stood four deep. The coach had wanted a quiet, closed practice to open preparation for the Green Bay game, but demands were such that at last he had to cave in to the pressures of publicity. All three networks were on hand, every magazine of any stature (*Life* assigned a poet and sculptor to capture the scene), plus huge numbers of personnel from the Voice of America and the armed-services press, and, of course, upward of a hundred members of the domestic United States newspaper corps, as well as representatives from papers in Canada, England, Australia, France, West Germany, and Japan.

The mayor showed up, bringing along the cardinal, a black Baptist minister, and a rabbi. Governor Agnew drove up from Annapolis. General Samuels and General Admire came over from the Pentagon, and the Army also donated to the Colts six public-information specialists, including a hot-shot colonel who had been flown all the way from Saigon. Then, at the last minute, just as Toby was finishing up posing for pictures with all the dignitaries, a huge helicopter loomed out of the sky and deposited itself on the far twenty-yard line. Vice-President Humphrey came bounding out, followed by the two Maryland senators, the NFL commissioner, Congressman Mendel Rivers of the House Armed Services Committee, and Marine Captain Chuck Robb, who just happened to be around since he was going to marry the President's daughter that same Saturday.

A half-hour later, when the Vice-President had concluded his few brief remarks, the helicopter lifted off again for Washington, and Toby was finally able to move out onto the practice field. He only shagged a few kickoff and punt returns, caught a few short passes from Unitas, and worked briefly in a reserve backfield on handoffs, but so much importance was attached to his every move that some reporters kept score, reporting to a breathless world exactly how many passes he caught, how many handoffs he juggled, and so on. When practice ended, all the reporters scurried upstairs to the press lounge for the official interview. Toby, all showered and dressed in civilian clothes, like an astronaut, entered the room with a Colt PR man on one side, while the Army PIO colonel from Saigon hung back only slightly on the other.

Toby swallowed and took the microphone, smiling out into the huge bank of color-TV lights. "Hey," he said with a big smile, "it was easier facing the Viet Cong than you gentlemen." And everyone laughed and rushed to jot down his *bon mot*. "How's it feel to be back, Toby?" one writer called out, and he replied, "Well, I'm used to action," and everybody really chuckled at that.

More questions, just as predictable, followed, most of them centering on what good shape he was in. Toby fielded them all smoothly, citing his rigorous Army training and pooh-poohing the shrapnel wounds that he had received in the combat action that won him the Congressional Medal. Admire and Samuels beamed. Uncle Sam whispered, "If our movie people get this stuff down right, we won't need any other recruiting bullshit for another year."

The line of questioning then turned to find out how familiar Toby was with his team, and with Green Bay's, how much he expected to play ("That's up to the coach"), was Unitas his boyhood idol (yes indeed), and was it a thrill to play with him? Toby answered, "Yes sir, it's a great thrill, and I don't think anything in my life has matched it except when I went into combat with the brave men I had the privilege of serving with in Vietnam." This reply so excited Admire and Samuels that they both shifted feet at the same time, and banged up against each other's Ranger Patches.

Then, off to a side, the man with a fluffy red beard from the Insight team of the London *Sunday Times* called out, "Major?" Just that one word brought a quick silence. Everyone else had addressed him as just Toby. Besides, obviously, the man with the beard had a decided accent, which suggested that his readers did not give a rat's ass about whether or not the Colts won the Coastal Division on Saturday.

"Major?"

"Yes sir?"

"Major Geyser, it has been suggested in some quarters that your return to the arena, shall we say, is merely a public-relations gimmick cooked up by the Army to help divert criticism of the war in Vietnam, and—"

"Yes," Toby said. His mind was racing.

"—well, particularly considering the rather rising flood of opinion directed against the US bombing of the North."

"Is that a question?"

"No, I'll provide two specific questions, Major," the beard said. "First, who inspired this idea, and second, do you believe that the United States government is using your popularity and celebrity to counter the anti-war criticism?"

Toby prayed that the panic that had crawled into his stomach was not surfacing on his face. Besides, for the first time he could feel little droplets of sweat from the television lights trickling down his face, but he did not dare reach up and brush them away. If he did, he was sure that it would appear that he was sweating from the question. So, agonized by the question, but tickled by the sweat, he tried to keep his face straight and answer. "First of all," he said, lying flat out, "the idea was strictly mine. I've been in a real war, and this is just a chance for me to play a game I love. The Colts are my team. They aren't just some team that drafted me. I grew up in this town. I've come home to play some football. It has nothing to do with the war we're fighting to save Vietnam and all Southeast Asia from a Communist takeover."

"But Major Geyser the war hero cannot be separated from Toby Geyser the All-American, can he?" the beard asked. "Are you a professional soldier or are you a professional football-player?"

"Well, right now I guess I'm both," Toby said, trying to smile a little to reduce the seriousness of the question. "But I'm not both at the same time. I'm a soldier playing football on his furlough. And after my furlough I'm assigned on a temporary consultant basis with the Maryland National Guard. I'm sure if the Colts win this Saturday and go on to the NFL championship and the Super Bowl even, I can get some time off from that assignment."

"So you acknowledge, Major, that you're getting special handling?"

For the first time Toby bristled and glared at the man. This

guy had it all figured out. "Special handling?" Toby replied, a
real cutting edge to his voice. "If I'm getting special handling
I wish somebody'd told that to the Viet Cong before they shot
me full of metal and killed half my platoon."

He drew a hard breath, expecting the beard to come right
back at him, but he had no chance, for suddenly some of the
sports press started applauding at the answer, and others made
grateful murmur noises. "Thanks, Toby," he heard someone
say, and they all melted before him, scurrying off to their type-
writers. The man from the New York *Daily News* flipped a
Western Union copy sheet in and began:

> Major Toby Geyser still has a crucial football game
> to play Saturday, but today the Vietnam hero made first
> down on his long touchdown march to Chief of Staff of
> the United States Army.
> First, on the practice gridiron, Geyser dispelled all doubts,
> looking every inch the All-American he was five years ago
> at West Point. Then, before a packed press conference,
> the clean-cut 27-year-old former Heisman Trophy winner
> displayed the kind of guts and . . ."

By the time these words were written, Toby was already pushing out of the press room, past the reporters who were patting
him on the back and saying, "Way to go, Toby," and, "Get
'em Saturday, Toby." General Samuels shoved aside three reporters and a sound man to reach him. He clasped his arm and
told him, "You showed that bearded Commie pansy."

"Yes sir," Toby replied, not stopping. "Thank you, sir." And
he pulled himself away from Unc Sam and found himself free.
For the first time he had a chance to wipe the sweat off his
brow, taking the whole arm of his coat and dragging it all over
his face. He could still hear one public-information officer
screaming after him about the special individual TV interviews,

but he kept on moving as if he didn't hear, and when he got down the ramps to the parking lot, he made a dash for his car and had backed it around and was disappearing into the traffic going west on 33rd Street just as the whole crew from ABC came chugging down the last ramp.

"A strategic retreat on the part of the heralded major," declared the announcer, a hawk-faced man with a cigarette between his lips, "but I am a veritable authority on tactics myself, and we shall outflank the incipient MacArthur with a rear-guard action that will make a cul-de-sac of his own bivouac."

"You mean go to his hotel?" the cameraman asked.

"Incredible," the announcer said. "I see that mere proximity to me is ameliorating this man's intellect." And, outlining the large part that he had personally played in the defeat of the Axis, he led his crew off to confront Toby at the Sheraton-Belvedere Hotel.

Toby himself drove aimlessly, turning north off 33rd onto Charles Street, heading in the opposite direction from the Sheraton-Belvedere. Suddenly he felt cool and relaxed at the wheel, and very smug. He understood at last that what pleased him so was how effective a liar he was. It had been so easy, and he had never been much good at it before. He flipped on the car radio. Toby had not been in Baltimore for eight years, but his fingers moved unconsciously to all his favorite old spots on the dial, as if they had memories of their own. He seemed to be driving the same way. He could not stop thinking about how well he had lied.

What surprised him most was how much easier it was to lie in public than to commit an everyday, private kind of lie. For instance, he thought, as he drove past the city limits at the Elkridge Club golf course, suppose he was with a girl and trying to get in her pants, and she said something such as Is This All You Want? he would answer, Of Course This Isn't All I Want.

That was, of course, every bit as blatant a lie as those he had told the beard, but the difference was that the girl would keep after him. She would say Are You Sure? or Do You Really Mean That? or Do You Promise Me That? and so on and so forth at great length. Once you lied and it was on TV, not only did everyone accept your claim right away, but it was absolutely certified just because it was on TV. Toby did not think that was fair. He thought that all press conferences should have just some of the girls he had encountered along the way, just asking, Really, Do You Mean That? or You're Not Just Saying That, Are You? or Are You Really Telling Me the Truth?

He was just buzzing along now, punching the buttons on the radio each time a commercial came on, without even thinking where he was heading, except that obviously he was not going in the direction of the Sheraton-Belvedere Hotel, to curl up with his secret looseleaf book of Colt plays and signals. At last he decided that since he was well into the suburbs, almost to Towson, he must be going to see Reds Ritchie at his house. Of course Toby was not going there at all, even if Reds had been home in the middle of the day, which he was not, and even if he still did live with his parents, which he did not. Of course Toby was cutting over to Ruxton to go to Rosalie's.

The house surprised him. It was much larger than he expected, a spacious red-brick colonial that was set back comfortably from the road, hidden among maple trees, and with a whitewashed fence around the whole property, so that it even resembled one of the fancy horse farms out in the Valley. "How can a dumb shit like Jerry Start afford a house like this?" Toby said out loud in the car. Toby didn't know about Cut 'N' Run; he had a total of $1784 in the bank himself, plus his GI insurance policy.

Toby had never, in his own mind, taken it out on Jerry for marrying Rosalie. Somebody was going to; it might just as well

have been his old buddy Jerry. Toby thought of Jerry sometimes as sort of a caretaker government for Rosalie. Even when
he first heard that she was pregnant, it never seriously entered
his mind that this had come about as a result of sexual inter-
course. He assumed, more or less, that it was just artificial in-
semination or immaculate conception—something along those
lines.

He parked the car a little bit farther down the road and started
walking back to the house. The Starts' kids, that is, Rosalie's
kids, the ones a stork had brought, were playing in a wire-fenced
circular area inside the yard. It was a bright, warm day for that
time of year, almost into December, but they were all bundled
up in about seventy-two snowsuits. The little boy had a plastic
yellow car that he was running over the little girl's legs with.
Toby said, "Hi." The little girl bobbled in his direction, but the
boy stood back and eyed him. "I'm Toby," he explained. "Is
your mother in? I mean, is your mother or father in?"

The little girl made some noises, something to do with water
or automobiles, one or the other, but little Jerry didn't say anything at all, so Toby walked around them toward the side door,
which was obviously the one everyone used. The Army is about
the only place left where people still use the front door.

Toby intended to ring the bell, but then he saw that the door
was open and he heard music playing, so he just pushed on
inside to the family room. The place was filled with galoshes,
but Rosalie wasn't there, so Toby followed the music. He recognized it as Billy Vaughan and his orchestra playing "Sail
Along, Silvery Moon." Billy Vaughan was very big in the fifties.
In fact, whenever Toby and Rosalie made out at her house, they
usually did it to Billy Vaughan, as it was a safe kind of music. It
was a bunch of saxophones or licorice sticks, one of those things
that just sort of hummed along in tune. If it was just a whole
lot of feeling around you were going to do, which was absolutely

all you could do in Rosalie's house, with her mother upstairs tuned in like a wiretap, and Rosalie set in a careful perimeter defense, then Billy Vaughan was the guy to do it to. He was perfect for endurance making out. His music lost popularity as soon as kids all started screwing one another in large quantities, as soon as that became the vogue in the sixties.

Toby followed the music, drawn to its source. This took him through the kitchen to the door to the basement den. It was wide open, so naturally he just stepped down the few steps to where he could look into the room below. There, at last, he saw Rosalie. She was on the rug by the color TV set, doing exercises in nothing but her panties.

12

Fly Pattern

The music was loud enough so that Rosalie couldn't hear anything except her own oomphs, which she released as she pulled herself up, stretching her stomach tight. Toby froze at the sight, and though she had absolutely nothing on but the panties, what he really stared at was her hair. He had always preferred her in a ponytail, which could make her so innocent or impudent, depending on how she flipped it, and he still remembered her that way. Now he was confronted by long, flowing locks that would spread out all over the rug when she drew back, then rear up in a wave as she stretched forward and said oomph.

As for her tits, he was merely intrigued by the perspective. God knows Toby was familiar enough with Rosalie's tits, having manipulated them, like the buttons on his car radio, for a sustained period of two years, but it occurred to him that this was an altogether new experience for him. Always before, he had seen her breasts only in the pitch dark of a car. If it had been one of those TV shows, *Truth or Consequences* or one of

that sort, and they had put Rosalie and some other girls behind
a big board with just their bare boobs sticking out, Toby
doubted whether he could guess the right pair in the bright
lights and from any respectable distance. On the other hand,
in the dark and close up, he was sure that he would have no
problem picking Rosalie's out, even if she was put up against,
say, the whole of the June Taylor Dancers, or any large group.

Suddenly Rosalie sensed that she was being watched and,
purposefully, before she dared look up and confirm her awful
feeling, she took her arms and crossed them over her chest,
grabbing each of her biceps with the fingers of her other hand.
It was a gesture of fright more than of modesty. Then she
raised her head slowly, gasping when she saw the man's feet.
The song on the LP ended, Billy Vaughan's orchestra petering
out to nowhere, and in that moment, on the silent grooves
between songs, she heard the man say, "I'm sorry, Rosie." Only
one person had ever called her that.

She dropped her arms to her sides and stared at him. Rain-
bows came out in her eyes, bells played in her head, little elves
ran about her body, sprinkling it with stardust, and her heart
beat so fast that she was sure that her left breast rose and fell,
like the tides. Billy Vaughan's orchestra began its rendition of
"Tumbling Tumbleweed." Rosalie was not excited that she was
seeing Toby for the first time in almost a decade. She was seeing Toby as she always had.

Reading from bottom to top, he had on Bass Weejuns, dark
woolen socks, cuffed charcoal-gray pants, a nondescript leather
belt, a dark brown tweed sports jacket, a button-down blue
oxford shirt with a navy blue and maroon regimental-stripe tie.
As the papers said, he stood six feet two and weighed 195. At
the age of sixteen, the day he discovered her after she had grown
up overnight, Toby Geyser stood six feet two and weighed 195.
His hair was the same color of so-what brown, and in the same

crew-cut style. It was eerie: he was even carrying a looseleaf notebook. There was nothing about him changed. It was as if he had stepped out for a milkshake and come back eight years later with the chocolate foam still on his lips. "Oh, it's you, Toby," she said.

For Rosalie, there was no Jerry Start, no Mrs. Start, no children, no President Kennedy, no Lee Harvey Oswald, no Vietnam, no Sweet Briar. She is not in any club cellar, because she must be home, and her father has all his guns in the club cellar. She must be up in the living room of her house, that of her parents, and she is certainly not sitting there in her panties, but has on a McMullen blouse, with a circle pin on the Peter Pan collar which is visible outside her favorite green crew-neck sweater. She is wearing a straight plaid wool skirt, with knee socks and loafers, because Toby is here to take her downtown to a first-run movie. Her number is VAlley 3-4288, because the exchanges still have names.

"Hi," he said.

"Hi."

He came down the stairs only a step at a time, stopping at the bottom long enough to put his Colt looseleaf down on a chair. He kept staring at her all the while, never taking his eyes from her face until he was close enough for her boobs to come back into their old clear focus. He touched them first only because they were the part of her closest to him. Then, going fairly berserk, he reached behind her and just sort of lifted her up off the ground, kissing her and pawing her. He was sort of leaning over her, stooped, so that she could not possibly stand up straight, but he was too involved in kissing her and yanking at her panties to stop and work out the arrangement so that it had more structural integrity.

Rosalie was of little value to the enterprise, since she just was hanging on for dear life. He jiggled her enough to drop her panties to her knees, but they caught there, and Rosalie pulled back enough to say, "No, no, not here." She must have whispered that refrain to Toby every night they ever went out, which was most of them for nearly two years. It was nearly obligatory for a girl at that time to say, "No, no, not here." It was a nice way of saying absolutely no, without seeming to, because where you were was the only available location. Usually it was a parked car. There were no Holiday Inns then, and at that time parents were also still dead set against kids screwing in the living room.

This time, however, Rosalie and Toby were not at the Timonium Drive-In Theatre or parked at Parton's. When she said, "No, no, not here," Toby just started looking around for another site. As he had noticed, it was a house with a lot of rooms. Other matters were flying around in Rosalie's mind. She remembered that, while it was still Toby from many years ago, she also had kids playing outside and a husband somewhere. And where was Jerry? There was something about her husband's whereabouts that she should know. Toby was almost dragging her to the nearest door by now. She couldn't walk because the panties were twisted about her knees, and he was required to jump along because his pants had dropped around his ankles and got caught on his Bass Weejuns. "Tumbling Tumbleweed" was rolling along.

Her husband, her husband, what was it about her husband? Rosalie knew it was something. Toby was fumbling with the doorknob by now and was dangerously close to kicking his Bass Weejuns off. Of course, Rosalie remembered, her husband had his National Guard meeting Tuesday nights, and then his APBA football league that followed well into the night. Her husband would not be home until almost morning. Therefore this was not a schedule conflict, but only a moral one. So immediately she took hold of his underpants and began to haul them down.

Toby turned the doorknob and pushed the door open. He saw in the dark that it was some kind of furnace room, but it looked clean enough, and accommodations were not uppermost in his mind. He shook off his shoes and stepped out of his pants, and Rosalie wiggled her panties down over her knees. He could tell that she did not care where they were so long as they got right about it.

Rosalie felt relaxed, even serene. She had enjoyed regular fantasies about this sort of thing, often even involving Toby, or sometimes Paul Newman or Al Martino. Of course, on those occasions Toby or Paul Newman or Al Martino would have to talk to her at length before she gave in to their entreaties. Paul Newman usually had to point out to Rosalie, for instance, that he was happily married, just as she was, and that he had the same normal extramarital guilt agonies gnawing at him.

"I just don't want to do anything to hurt Joanne," Rosalie would sob, pulling away from his advances.

"God, neither do I," Paul Newman would reply. "And I don't want to hurt Jerry. But is it fair for us to hurt ourselves?"

And then, always, Rosalie would kiss his blue eyes shut and reach for the top button on her blouse. "I want this to be just right for both of us," she would say.

As for Al Martino, Rosalie was unfamiliar with his marital status, and she would give in to him only after he employed a ships-passing-in-the-night argument and sang to her a little. Yet in these dreams Toby was hardest of them all to turn down, inasmuch as his desire for her had a patriotic ring to it. He was always just about to embark on another tour of Vietnam, explaining that he had never let her stray from his mind the whole first time he had been over there. These fantasies with Toby were expanded somewhat to include deep philosophical discussions about the merits of the bombing, but in the end Rosalie always decided that there were fairer and more effective ways to express her opposition of the bombing than by withholding her body from one poor soldier boy. In any event, on no occasion in any of these dreams did either Toby, Paul Newman, or Al Martino sneak into the house like a peeping Tom and then carry her off panting to the furnace room.

Rosalie raised no protest, however, simply because she believed that this was her due. Sexwise, Rosalie figured that her crowd had gotten the worst of it. She had been brought up to defend her honor. Not only was she taught that this was right, but she was also assured that it was wise, inasmuch as virtue was a vital male consideration in the selection of a permanent mate. Rosalie played hard by these rules, nearly driving herself and Toby loony in the process, and the guy she finally did marry anyway had been firmly convinced all along that she had been screwing for years. Moreover, worst of all, as soon as Rosalie made it safely across the finish line, into Jerry's bed alone, every girl in America started laying all over, and none the worse for it. Was this fair?

Rosalie was the oldest in her family. She had a younger sister, Marcy, who was just now a high-school senior, and Rosalie knew for a fact that Marcy had been getting it for years. But then, Marcy was the picture of health, popular with girls and boys alike, head of the Youth Fellowship at church, and an A student. Also, Marcy could go swimming thirty-one days a month and certainly did not appear to have reduced marital prospects. At the age of seventeen, Marcy knew more about men than Rosalie ever would, and here she was already with one boob in the grave.

What really killed Rosalie about it most was her mother. She had sniffed around Toby and her like a hound dog and evicted him from the house for two weeks just because she caught them French kissing a little while they were watching TV. Mrs. Totter then gave Rosalie a copy of *'Twixt Twelve and Twenty* by Pat Boone, with this passage underlined in red: *"Kissing for fun is like playing with a beautiful candle in a roomful of dynamite. I really think it's better to amuse ourselves in some other way. I say go bowling, or to a basketball game."*

Then this same woman had come over to see Rosalie just a couple of weeks ago and said, "I just hope Marcy is playing it as safe with Rudy as she did with Tod and the fellow at the beach. I'd feel so much better if she'd go to Dr. Stallings and get some pills or a good diaphragm, you know?" So Rosalie believed that neither Toby nor anybody else would qualify her for adultery or anything of that nature. She would merely be getting what she deserved on a delayed basis.

And certainly it was imminent. Toby spied a rug over in the far corner by the washing machine and dragged Rosalie toward it. By now, having settled all philosophical conundrums, Rosalie was really in the spirit of things too. She was kissing Toby's ear and his neck, and scratching at his back. She had pulled his undershirt up around his neck. Entwined, mad for each other, they slumped to the rug, panting, grabbing, ready for each other at last.

"Oh my God, Toby, noooo," Rosalie screamed in that instant, and she was gone. In a burst of incredible strength, she rose up with such force that she threw Toby off her. All of a sudden Toby was lying there in a daze on his back, while Rosalie was standing straight up. Toby was so baffled by it all that he could feel goosepimples running up and down his spine.

"Hey," he said.

"Why did you bring me in here?"

"Because where we were, you said, 'No, no, not here.' "

"I did?"

"Well, you always did. Only before, I never had any alternatives."

"Then it was a bad mistake," Rosalie said, and she groped

around in the air for the cord to pull the light on. "Look, we've got Bingo Turf all over us." She turned halfway to show him all the little green things imbedded in her, from her calves up to her shoulder blades. She looked as if she had green blackheads. "Oh, Toby, we finally get to make it, and you have to go try and screw in the Bingo Turf."

13

Audibles

"What the hell is Bingo Turf?" Toby asked.

"It's like AstroTurf, only it doesn't work," Rosalie explained. She had cleared off Jerry's desk, thrown a couple of towels over it, and had laid herself down across it, like a patient. Toby, wielding a pair of tweezers, was standing over her.

"I never really ever saw your heinie before," he said.

"I get enough play-by-play around here, if you don't mind."

"Well, it was just a polite observation, sort of an icebreaker," he said quickly. He dug in with the tweezers and pulled a couple of the green fibers out.

"Couldn't you at least put your underpants on, doctor?" Rosalie asked. "You keep brushing up against me when you lean over to operate. It's very distracting."

"I tried to get into them while you were getting the tweezers," Toby said. "But they just make the Bingo Turf hurt more. This stuff is really brutal."

"We had to take the schnauzer to the vet's when he got into it."

"What do you keep the stuff around for?"

"Owww!" Rosalie screamed. "For God's sake, Toby, stop talking and watch what you're doing."

"I'm sorry. This isn't easy, you know." Gingerly he went after some Bingo Turf that was really deeply imbedded and pinched her skin again in the process. "Ooops."

"Owww! Damn it, Toby, what do you think you're on, one of your search-and-destroy missions?"

"You're in no position—there, I got it—you're in no position to make any snide anti-war remarks."

"Oh, I'm not?" She raised up on her elbows and turned her head around to look at him. Unfortunately for Rosalie, this left her staring dead ahead at Toby's private parts, which was disconcerting. Besides, she wanted to keep this on a high plane. So she turned around the other way and stretched her neck to see him. "Oh no, and who's going to take the Bingo Turf out of your fanny if I don't—Johnny Unitas?"

"That's a good point. Touché," Toby said, and Rosalie flipped him the peace sign before laying her face back down on her forearms. In return, he spanked her two times, though being kind enough to hit her only on the cheek where he had removed all the Bingo Turf already.

"That's just the kind of response I would expect from a man committed to violence," Rosalie said out of the side of her mouth.

"Goddamn it, Rosie, cut that crap out. I'm sick of everybody getting on my back. Everybody snickers at my hair. No girls short of menopause and east of the Alleghenies will go out with me. I stop in somewhere for a friendly beer and have to spend the next two hours defending the bombing. It's worse than being a colored person and having to talk about race all the time. I wouldn't dare wear my uniform off base any more—there, I got that little devil out too."

"Nobody made you become a soldier."

"Oh, for Chrissakes, Rosie, do you really think that the prospect of spending another year getting shot at in that godforsaken place pleases me? There, that's the last one on your big boomy." Toby cruised over it with his hand. "No, wait a minute. Here's one more. What really bugs me is that everyone I meet, like you, is so damn smug about it. Everybody has all the answers."

"Owww!"

"There, I got it. It's so easy, so pat. And what really kills me, everybody gets worked up only when it's convenient, when they're through babbling about pro football and the market—"

"Hey, that's my husband you're defaming," Rosalie said.

"Oh hell, I don't mean Jerry. I mean every goddamn body. It's the truth. I noticed this as soon as I got back. People talk about Vietnam like it was a losing streak or a dip in the Dow-Jones averages or some damn thing. They talk about it like somebody just fumbled. I swear to God, Rosie, if we don't win the war soon—"

"Hear, hear!"

"I said if. I swear, some historian will look back one hundred years from now and say it was all on account of the pro football mentality. It's all Colts and Rams and bulls and bears and bombers and guerrillas. It's all the same back here, another big dumb ball game. What really pisses everybody off is that they can't get a final score. That's all." He patted her affectionately on the rear. "I'm almost done."

"Good," Rosalie said, "because before I start on you, I've got to get the kids in for their dinner."

"Oh my God, I forgot all about them."

"It is apparent that you did not bring to bear a lot of planning on this little foray of yours."

"Suppose the kids came in while we were like this?" Toby asked, suddenly concerned at the possibility.

"No problem," Rosalie said. "I'd just give them the same excuse as last week when they caught me down here with the laundryman."

"Oh, for God's sake, Rosie, they could tell Jerry."

"Toby, they could tell General Westmoreland. They could tell Walter Cronkite," Rosalie said, turning around again. "But can you imagine them getting this scene across to anybody? We got a four-year-old and a two-year-old talking pidgin English, saying, 'General Westmoreland, Major Geyser was down in our club cellar the other afternoon, standing there naked as a jaybird, pulling Bingo Turf out of Mrs. Start's derrière with a pair of tweezers.'"

"Well—"

"Besides, Jerry is so worked up about the game Saturday that I don't believe he would take any notice if he caught us screwing in his office at high noon."

"I hope you're right. There, that's the last one," he said, patting a spot up around her shoulders.

"Okay, lie down real quick, and I'll try to get you done." Rosalie jumped up, retrieved her panties from the utility room, and slipped on the wrapper she had worn downstairs before starting her exercises. "I don't think you've got as many as I did," she said.

"Well, you know," Toby said, lying down across the desk. "I was pressing down on you."

"I don't think it is necessary to draw diagrams, Toby."

"Hell—owww, that hurts—you're the one that's so blasé about all this."

"Well, now," Rosalie said, drumming the tweezers on his rear, "did you really expect to come back and find that same wide-eyed high-school virgin with a ponytail?"

Toby pondered that a second. "Mmm-huh," he said, "yes, in a way, I guess I did expect that."

"Well, I suppose that's sweet of you," Rosalie said, "but then, all our generation ever had was fantasies anyhow."

"And what does that mean?"

"Oh, you know. Boy, this one is really in there. We were all such frivolous, insincere kids. I can see it now, how silly my life was. I've learned so much from today's young people. They're so honest, so relevant, so real, so—"

Toby raised himself up on his elbows and turned around and, notwithstanding that one breast was peeking out from the folds of her robe, looked Rosalie straight in the eye. "Rosalie Totter eats it on a stick," he said.

She giggled. "I haven't heard anybody say that in years," she said.

"I was saving it for somebody who really deserves it. Do you really mean to tell me that you've fallen for all this nickel-dime worship of this modern younger generation?"

"Oh come on, Toby, you know they're so much smarter and more sensitive than we ever were. They're so down-to-earth. They don't have all the sexual hang-ups we had."

"Sexual hang-ups?" Toby screamed. "Who the hell had sexual hang-ups? Christ knows I tried to screw you every chance I got."

"Well, the girls don't have any sexual hang-ups."

"So everybody fucks like a bunny—this qualifies them for having all the answers? Everybody says they're so idealistic. That poor Carla Poole, the one with a dirty blouse all the time; I guess she could be archbishop, she was so damn idealistic."

"You're just mad because they see through the immorality of your war."

"Rosie, they just don't want their heads blown off. Hell, I don't blame them for that."

"Oh, Toby, you're still trapped in the hypocritical morass of the nineteen-fifties."

"A pig's ass," Toby said. "They don't want their heads blown off."

"You're just being sarcastic. They're so much better than we were—concerned, not apathetic. Full of love, not bias and cruelty. They're such fine young people."

"Goddamn it, I can't take that," Toby said, and he sprang up from the desk and stalked away.

"Hey, I'm not through," Rosalie said, waving her tweezers.

"I just got to stand up a minute. What a lot of crap."

"What are you so worked up about?"

"It pisses me off. It's bad enough that nobody in my generation got laid. But that we got to be bad-mouthed too." Toby was pacing back and forth, not really mindful of the fact that he didn't have any clothes on. "Now, what was that last thing you called them?"

"The younger generation?"

"Yeah. What did you call them?"

"Relevant?"

"No, not that," Toby cried. "You already did that. You called them young people. That's what you called them."

"I guess."

"Listen, when you were a kid, did anybody ever call you a young people? You damn right they never did. They called us kids and teens and youngsters, for Chrissake, youngsters, and you guys. Nobody ever dignified us by calling us young people."

"I guess you're right," Rosalie said, sitting up on the desk.

"Now, though, all these kids, hey, they're young people and treated with deference. What a bunch of frauds. The only thing different about this generation is that they all get laid and they got good public relations."

"*Time* magazine made them Man of the Year last year," Rosalie told him.

"The young people?"

"Yeah. I guess you were in Vietnam then."

"You see," Toby cried. "The media have swallowed all this garbage. All everybody does is go around interviewing them.

Obtain the views of the young people. Did anybody ever obtain my view when I was a young people? Hell, no. They just
kept telling us that we were apathetic. All the time—apathy
this, apathy that. And then the other experts would step in
and say, Well, no wonder the stupid kids are so apathetic, because, poor things, they were the first ones ever to be brought
up in the shadow of the atom bomb. Everybody said that. If
some kid wet his bed or didn't turn his homework in, everybody said, Well, what do you expect, he was the first generation
brought up in the shadow of the atom bomb. I never thought
five minutes in my whole life about being brought up in the
shadow of the atom bomb. Nobody did. Did you?"

"Of course not."

"Right." Toby pounded his hands like a lawyer. "But the experts who decided on that piece of bullshit are the same ones
that also say that the kids getting laid all the time now are
idealistic, but we were apathetic. Who's apathetic anyway? Now
you think about the young people nowadays. They don't have
to go to class and now they're cutting out grades too, because
they're not relevant. Nobody cares whether you drink—"

"They're smoking marijuana now."

"Okay, same thing. The point is, it's okay, drinking or
smoking. And everybody screws on sight. You don't have to
cut your hair or wash it, you don't have to change clothes, and
you don't even have to learn how to dance. For Chrissake,
when I was a young people I had to spend all my time learning
how to do all those damn dances."

"I guess that's right," Rosalie said.

"You're damn right. You wouldn't even rate a good feel unless you could do all the new dances. And I had to get up and
go to class and try to get good grades. And then I had to get
haircuts and shop for new chinos all the time, and then I had
to start mousing around with you. It was hours just to qualify

for a little dry humping. Christ, the time I took just getting your bra off, if I'd had that free time, you know, accumulated over the years, I could have learned to speak Chinese, I could have written a great opera or something.

"Apathetic, hell, it took me a full day's work the way the rules were set up. Me and my friends, my generation, we had to spend all the time left over when we weren't learning dances at least trying to break the rules. These kids nowadays, the young people, they don't have any rules to break. They don't have any imagination. If they don't like something, they just don't do it. Which is idealistic, of course.

"They get up in the morning. They put the same clothes on. The girls don't have to do their hair or put a bra on or anything. The boys don't have to shave. Look, I'd rather have a period once a month than have to shave every day. So they get up, they wander over to school in their new cars and tell the teachers how everybody else is hypocritical, then they break for a few drinks or some smokes and get a quick screw—and it's still only half past one in the afternoon. So they spend the rest of the day being young people and letting experts obtain their views on how sincere and idealistic they are."

"Oh, stop it, Toby," Rosalie said, laughing. "I never thought of it like that."

"I know," Toby said. "It's the greatest fraud in history."

"I've got to go outside and get the kids now," Rosalie said. "I'll come back and finish de-Bingo Turfing you as soon as I get them fed."

"Okay," Toby said, and he picked up his Colt play book and lay back down on the desk and studied it. Especially he concentrated on the end runs and off-tackle slants he might be running if the coach used him at set back. Rosalie came back in a little while and began to complete the extraction process, while the two children shuffled partway down the steps and sat there and watched. It was a very domestic scene, but after a while Jerry Jr. and Kimberly got tired of watching Rosalie yank Bingo Turf out of Toby's right rear, so they went back upstairs and watched television. Toby had most of the off-tackle plays down pat by the time Rosalie got the last of the Bingo Turf out of him.

14

Trap Play

Toby should have expected, even before he arrived back at the Sheraton-Belvedere, that his whereabouts was bound to leak out eventually. Still, in no way could he have been prepared for the scene that greeted him as he casually pushed through the revolving doors into the hotel lobby. There were hordes of people, children and grown-ups alike, on hand, all brandishing autograph books and Kodak cameras. Others were waving banners and homemade signs, and one whole side of the room was lined with disabled Vietnam veterans in wheelchairs. There were tons of electronic gear, all of which suddenly became activated and started whirring as soon as Toby came through the door. Worst of all, a whole legion of men in blazers zeroed in on him from all directions, shoving microphones into his face.

The hawk-nosed man from ABC, rattling the rib cages of his competitors with his pointed elbows, reached Toby first and neatly maneuvered him backward behind the newsstand counter. All of a sudden the ABC camera pushed the poor little newsstand lady aside and began rolling. "Major Toby Geyser," the commentator announced in a gravelly voice, "speaking to me in his first exclusive US interview. If you will, and I'm sure you will, forgive the intrusion of a *soupçon* of hyperbole: the true modern Renaissance Man. Hero and idol, scholar and leader, these things are the young gentleman who is also warrior and athlete. As he brings to this rare confidential conversation the same grace and command that marks either of his vocations, on the battlefield or on the playing field. Major Toby Geyser, Congressional Medal of Honor winner, speaking to us exclusively, a figure larger than life, one who wears the epaulettes, figuratively, of Ike Eisenhower and Doug MacArthur, of Black Jack Pershing and Zachary Taylor, of Grant and Lee, yes them both, for though they held opposing commands across the nation's bleeding gulf, they were schooled in that same repository of intellect and honor on the Hudson that now gives us this brightest symbol of youth and leadership. We'll be back in just one minute." The lights went off. "Hold tight, Toby, you're doing great. The commercial goes in here.

"All right, let's pick it back up," the announcer said after a few more seconds. The lights went back on. "We continue our fascinating, and very revealing, exclusive interview with Major Toby Geyser. And so the question before us is, can he trade one uniform for another, can he come back to the city of his nativity—was Thomas Wolfe right when he said, you can't come home again?—can he, the hunter, return to his hill, to try and bring the Baltimore Colts an upset victory over their most vaunted Nemesis, the powerful Pack from Green Bay, Wisconsin, and victory in the rugged Coastal Conference of the NFL? A tough assignment, Major."

"It certainly is," Toby said.

The announcer nodded solemnly. "So succinctly phrased, and yet, as we have come to expect from this unique young man, so characteristically modest and bold, one and the same. And so, here he is, Toby Geyser, back in his home town, the city of Baltimore, Maryland, the Monumental City, the sixth largest in the nation, resting not by the Chesapeake Bay, as is so commonly imagined, but by that mighty inlet's tributary, the Patapsco River, playing for his beloved Colts, arrayed against what is considered the most efficient and awesome football machine ever assembled. All right, Major, what makes you so confident that you can single-handedly take the Packers apart?"

"What?" said Toby.

"We'll be back in just a minute with a final word," said the announcer. Thereafter, in all the other exclusive interviews, Toby just said, "Great," as regularly as he could. It was great to be back, great to be playing, great to be playing for the Colts, great to be playing against the Packers; this reception was great. Then he went over and began shaking hands with the wounded soldiers, who apparently had been bused over from Walter Reed Hospital on the orders of DANG and DONG, under the impression that they were going to meet Blaze Starr stripteasing down on the Block.

With the soldiers, Toby dispensed dandy little homilies about the values of war and pro football every time a stray microphone was thrust into his face. Finally, as the cameras moved away, he was able to turn and face the autograph mobs and try to make his way to the elevators. He would just sign whatever was thrust at him and hold it up for the owner to retrieve. He did not even look up, except occasionally to make sure that he was still plowing the right course for the elevators. Another book came at him, and he grabbed it and started to sign it reflexively, when he saw that there was something already written on the green page that was held open for him. It was in large red block letters and was the one word: OVERLORD.

Toby looked up, trying to mask his surprise, and might have been good at it except that he found himself looking at a tall blonde. She was nearly beautiful, smartly dressed, and she smiled cunningly out from behind her big hornrimmed glasses. "My son has always been a great fan of yours, Major Geyser," she said stiffly, perfectly enunciating every syllable.

"Oh, yeah," Toby said. He retained enough presence of mind to write down his room number and pass the book back to her. "Thank you, Major," she said and faded away into the mob. It was almost another half-hour before Toby had signed all the autographs, picked up his messages, and retreated to his room.

She was standing there when he came out of the bathroom. "You're pretty tricky," Toby said. "How did you get in?"

The blonde smiled and held up some kind of large wonder key and nodded toward a door on the other side of the room. "I'm your next-door neighbor."

"What a revoltin' development this is," Toby said, remembering to zip up his fly too. He slumped down on his bed, kicked his loafers off, and beckoned her to take a chair. She sat down and folded her legs neatly, primly, crossing them at her ankles to the side, like a beauty-pageant contestant. Toby did not really notice this, however, because she had wonderfully rolling breasts, which quivered under her blouse. These explained why she did not have to wear contact lenses instead of the horn-rims to interest men. "Look, I'm really hungry," Toby said. "Can I order you something too?"

The blonde roared at this example of his abject stupidity. It was nearly a cackle. "Now, that wouldn't be very clever, Major," she said, speaking down to him. "There's only supposed to be one person in this room, and dinner for two might arouse suspicions."

"Suppose I got a large cherry Coke and two straws?"

"You'll be very big on the Johnny Carson Show, I'm sure," she replied. "Only this is not a social call."

"Well, don't be so mean," Toby said. "I'm new at this sort of thing. This whole business about DANG and DONG—"

"Major Geyser, please. No reference is ever to be made to those agencies, ever. Ever." Even though she had been ordering him about ever since she had come into the room, those words had a special new authority to them. They were clipped and frosty, and her eyes glared out in a lockstep. Toby thought that she must surely be a Lesbian.

"I forgot, I'm sorry," he said, "but get this straight. Whether you know it or not—"

"It's my business to know."

"Yeah, well, then maybe you also know that until the Colts' season is over, my primary mission is football."

"Yes, I know that. I just want you to do one thing for me."

"Do something! Look at these messages. I got about ten radio stations to call, I've got to get something to eat, and I've got a whole offense to learn in another four days."

"You had all afternoon to start on that, Major."

"Never mind what I choose to do with my time," Toby snapped. "Or are you tailing me?"

"I have no interest in your affairs," the blonde said, and Toby felt quite sure that she accented the last word for his benefit. "I just want to capture Tyrone Dancer before he blows up any more National Guard armories and skips the country. Is that clear, Major?"

"Hey, stop calling me Major."

"What do you want me to call you?"

"I don't know. It just seems to me that on a genuine under-cover mission I ought to have a good code name. Mr. X or the Scarlet Pimpernel or something. What are you?"

"I'm just Ginger," she said.

"Is that your real name or your spy name or what?"

"No, that's just my name. Ginger Toogood."

"That's a helluva name," Toby said, in real admiration.

"I was named after my uncle," Ginger explained. "I'm really Ginger Toogood the second, only of course girls aren't ever the second or junior or any such thing."

"Right," Toby said. This was the best part of the conversation, because he felt that he was really getting to know Ginger more as a person. He even began to seriously doubt if she were a Lesbian. In fact, Ginger's availability, her residence in the next room, encouraged Toby to conjure up some of the more intriguing ways in which they could while away a few hours every now and then. After all, every schoolchild knows that female spies are required to spend the bulk of their time performing the most spectacular acts of sexual legerdemain in order to get information out of high government officials, generals, and male spies. Toby began to appreciate that he had really stumbled onto a sexual bonanza. The potential was so obvious that it made him think that he was itching from Bingo Turf again. "Listen, Ginger Toogood," he said, "this is nothing fresh or anything, but I got a real itch in my back."

"I've got good long nails," Ginger said, and she came right over and sat down next to him on the bed and began to scratch.

"The only thing worse is having hiccups," Toby said.

"I never get hiccups," Ginger said, adjusting her scratching up and over to the left, to where Toby indicated the itching was. She was a fantastic scratcher. He just sat there and imagined what she could do, just in the realm of scratching, if he actually had a secret that she wanted. "I've never had hiccups in my life. Nobody in my family has ever had them."

"There are some people I've read about who—I mean these are just real normal ordinary everyday people—who get hiccups and have them for years and years and just waste away—"

"On account they can't keep any food down," Ginger said.

"Right? You've read about them too?"

"Oh, sure. How's that?"

Toby said it was fine, and Ginger stopped scratching and went back to her chair. By the time she was back there, Toby had the hiccups. Luckily, however, he did not maintain them for years on end. As a matter of fact, they stopped right away because Ginger suddenly stood up, kicked off her spike heels and undid the first two buttons on her blouse.

Toby gulped. Ginger buttoned them right back up. "I just scared you," she said. "That's how you get rid of hiccups—you scare people. I scared the hell out of you, didn't I?"

Toby agreed as how she had. This had to be one of the shrewdest women he had ever met in his life. "Ginger Toogood," he said, "you're my kind of spy."

"If I ever took off my glasses, you would discover that I'm a ravishing beauty too," she replied. Toby began to think that probably she was a clandestine nymphomaniac, holding herself in check. Obviously, if you are going to go around screwing all the important people with secrets, sooner or later you are going to go over the line. An awful lot of important people have secrets. As a consequence, Toby decided not to let on to Ginger that he knew any secrets—at least not right away. Far be it from him to push her over the brink, because he had learned to like her as a person.

So he just said, "All right, Ginger Toogood, what do you want me to do?"

"I want you to get in touch with Sandy Tatler at the National Guard right away."

"It can't wait a week?"

"No, and for a very good reason. Because I think Tyrone Dancer is ready to try to make it out of the country any day now. And I'm almost sure that Tatler knows where he's hiding. If we're going to catch Dancer, you've got to move on Tatler now."

"What do I do?"

"All I want you to do is drop by the Guard meeting tonight —it's over at the Fifth Regiment Armory—introduce yourself to Tatler, and get that friend of yours to invite Tatler and his wife to the party he's having for you tomorrow night."

"How the hell did you find out about Jerry's party?" Toby asked.

"It's hardly a guarded state secret," Ginger replied. Obviously, she had slept with somebody who was going to the party, and Toby wondered who. "I have my ways." She sighed, and her breasts heaved against her blouse. They reminded Toby of something. In the old comic strip *Smilin' Jack* there used to be a fat guy with a huge belly, who had a pet chicken who would follow him around. What this pet chicken did was, it gobbled up the buttons that were always bursting off the shirt that was stretched by the fat guy's huge belly. The chicken would actually catch these buttons right out of the air in its mouth and eat them. It subsisted on these buttons. This thought occurred to Toby, for Ginger Toogood's blouse buttons were straining mightily.

"Okay," Toby said, "because you scratched my back, I'll go see Tatler."

"And get him and his wife invited to that party tomorrow."

"Yes, ma'am, Ginger Toogood."

She slipped her shoes back on and stood up to leave. "And, Major, one more thing, just to save us both some embarrassment and yourself a letdown. Don't operate under the delusion that just because I'm a female spy you've stumbled onto some kind of sexual bonanza."

"Why would I think that?" Toby said. "That wouldn't even cross my mind."

"Well, I'm certainly glad to hear that," Ginger said. "It's a bum rap all of us in the field have to suffer just because of a few bad girls."

"Gee, that never would have even occurred to me," Toby said.

"Well, fine," Ginger said, going to the door to her room. "Then we won't even have to lock this."

"Of course not," Toby said, starting to itch from the Bingo Turf again. "Look, when you're on an undercover mission, I always say there's no time for any stuff like that."

"You're a real gentleman, Major. So many people just automatically stereotype girl spies as loose and easy women."

"I'm sure there's many ways to get secrets besides that," Toby said, most emphatically.

She blew him a kiss and opened the door. "Actually," Ginger Toogood said, "I have a very heavy beau who wants to take me away from all this."

15

On Any Given Day

Rosalie, in a half-slip, stood up before her bedroom mirror to admire herself. Then she draped her new pants suit over her body, and, after that, held up a couple of exceptionally short miniskirts. She was trying to decide what to wear for the party that evening that she and Jerry were giving for Toby. It was not an easy choice.

Several weeks before, Rosalie had gone to New York to visit her old roommate, Mary Beth Potter, for a weekend. Tom Potter was taking some special clients to Pittsburgh to watch the Giants play the Steelers. The Colts were scheduled to play the Forty-Niners at home that Sunday, and Jerry had been beside himself for the whole week in anticipation of the game. "You bet you can go to New York, Baby Cakes," he told Rosalie. "A MUST game like this one coming up, it's good for both of us that you can get away and have some silly girl talk."

The check for the sale of a hundred shares of Cut 'N' Run had just come in from the Richmond brokerage, so, when Jerry was memorizing all the predictions in his *Expert Pro Grid* news-letter one night while watching TV game highlights, Rosalie asked him if she could take some of that money and buy clothes in New York. Jerry replied with a comment about the lateral speed of interior linemen, which Rosalie accepted as an affirmative. She put $1500 of the Cut 'N' Run money in her checking account and went on a shopping spree with Mary Beth in all the wild new boutiques along Madison Avenue.

Even though the Colts beat the Forty-Niners in the MUST game, Jerry was furious with what Rosalie bought. He dismissed the pants suit as some kind of homosexual-inspired jet-set aberration. He used the miniskirts as proof that the Republic was sliding into depravity. Then Rosalie put on the see-through blouse. Of course, like most see-through blouses, this one was pretty tricky to see through. The see-througher had to be located exactly three and a half feet away from the see-throughee, looking up on an azimuth that was precisely north-by-northeast. Under those circumstances, in bright natural lighting, two small freckles of Rosalie's, on the underside of her right breast, just where it merged with the rib cage, could be clearly discerned. That was the see-through part. Naturally, because Rosalie was going to parade around virtually in the raw, Jerry lost complete control of himself, and she agreed to send the see-through back. In the bargain, as Rosalie had intended, he waived all rights to censor her other new clothes.

Rosalie had narrowed her party choice down between the red corduroy miniskirt, which Jerry characterized as sufficient "hardly to cover your twat," and the pants suit, which, though modest enough, was still also considered revolutionary apparel at that time. At last Rosalie decided on the pants suit, since she was sure that Jerry would be more upset if she wore the miniskirt in front of Toby. Satisfied with this crucial decision, she lay back on her bed and idly picked up a magazine.

It happened to be Jerry's latest copy of *Playboy*, and, flipping through it, Rosalie came upon a fascinating article. It was a story about Toni Winston, the former Vassar Phi Beta Kappa who had gone on to such great success in films. People occasionally told Rosalie that she looked a lot like Toni Winston. This article featured some startling nude pictures of Miss Winston from her soon-to-be-released film, *Sign of the Condor*, and explained why she had consented to be the first major American star to appear nude on the screen.

"When I first read the script," the stately former Ivy-legged coed told *Playboy*, "I was tremendously excited with the potential of this rare film statement. It was such a sensitive story, so tender, yet provocative, that I knew the film *was* me. At first I felt sure that the nude scene in the garage [from whence the film's haunting title] could be skipped, or that a stand-in could be used for European consumption. But soon, as I came to live the part, to really *be* Sheilah, I knew, *I knew*, that the very hypocrisy that the film exposes required that I be genuine if I were to discover the relevancy the whole cast was searching for."

Breathlessly Rosalie read on about how Toni Winston explained this to her husband, Producer Karl Anders, and to her parents, and how all of them understood immediately that nudity was just another form of expression. Rosalie found that to be the warmest part of the story, although she, like Toni, was relieved that the scene was filmed in tasteful privacy. In fact, the intrepid *Playboy* photographer was the only outsider allowed on the set.

Moments later, sitting next to Husband Anders, with a terry-cloth robe thrown about her bare shoulders, the shapely 39-23-37 chestnut-haired egghead told *Playboy* that "This morning, for the first time as an actress, I felt fulfilled!" Turn the page for a more educated study of the famous Toni magna cum body bountiful in the buff.

So it was that Rosalie was just putting on the red corduroy miniskirt when Jerry came home. "For Chrissake, it hardly covers your twat," he bellowed.

"If Toni Winston can parade around the wide screen in nothing but her Phi Beta Kappa key, I can certainly wear stylish clothing in my own house," Rosalie replied, picking up the tempo.

"I don't care what Toni Winston does. You're not a goddamn movie star."

"Oh, these aren't good enough for you," Rosalie cried, poking her breasts with her index fingers. Girls who grow up with big boobs always think that, as Hollywood instructed them as little girls, big boobs are crucial to their popularity. Only girls who must get by without big boobs ever find out the real truth, that size really doesn't count that much, that men are only mainly concerned with the correct number and location. Girls like Rosalie would descend into middle age much better if someone would only write a popular calypso chant on that subject. "You'd think you'd be proud of the way I look."

"Baby Cakes, I am proud," Jerry said, trying a new tack. "It's just that what others think—I mean, Glenda Fiola will have Cardinal Shehan himself over here after you if she gets a look at that. She started saying Hail Marys on the spot the night you just told her you took the Pill. And would you believe Karen O'Reilly is worse than her?"

"If Karen O'Reilly is upset it's because she couldn't fit her big can into one of these," Rosalie said. "If you don't care what Toni Winston does, I don't care what Karen O'Reilly does."

So that tack didn't work. So Jerry tried a new tack, which he introduced by cursing and throwing his socks. They hit the window shade, which made it fly up, which awakened Halfback with a start, and he set to yipping. "Well, if it was just

friends," Jerry screeched. "But you know, Toby's got the Tatlers coming over, for Chrissake. You watch, Rosalie, it'll be all
over niggertown."

"I wasn't aware that our standing in that community was of
any consequence to you," Rosalie said. "If the word gets around
to Bubba Smith and Lenny Moore, you'd be the proudest
husband in Baltimore."

Jerry cursed and kicked at his shoes. "One goddamn weekend in New York with Mary Beth," he yelled. "Never again.
You come back dressed like the town punchboard and talking
like a hippie. You're never going to New York alone again."

"If you paid any attention to me at all from July to January,
I wouldn't want to go to New York," Rosalie shouted back.
"This is the first time you've even noticed what I had on since
they started playing exhibitions."

"How many times do I have to tell you, they're not exhibitions, they're pre-season games?"

"Next year I'm going to get a big number 19 to wear on my
chest. Maybe if you thought I was Johnny Unitas, you might
at least call signals to me occasionally," Rosalie shrieked, leaning down to put on her heels.

"That just shows you how much you know," Jerry replied,
smirking. "It's Johnny Unitas who *calls* the signals. You don't
even know who calls the fucking signals."

Rosalie stood up, tossed her hair loose, reached for some
boutique beads, and pointed at Jerry. "Now I'm going downstairs to get things ready. Hurry up and help me. You know
we asked Toby to come early."

"You'd think after not seeing Toby for almost ten years
that you wouldn't want him to see you looking like a two-bit
whore," Jerry cried after her.

Rosalie stopped on the stairs. "Listen, Nutsy Fagan," she
said, "I spent two of the best years of my nubile young life

defending myself from Toby Geyser's most persistent and deft advances. If there is anybody on God's green earth who knows I'm no two-bit whore, it is Toby Geyser."

"Aww, buzz off," said Jerry.

Toby was, in fact, already standing outside on the porch, waiting for Rosalie and Jerry to stop shouting at each other so that he could ring the doorbell. He didn't want any trouble. He had not been pleased with how he had practiced that afternoon, and he was still scared that one of the children might recognize him, even though he had clothes on. When at last it grew quiet inside, he straightened his tie and rang the bell, but when Rosalie greeted him at the door in her miniskirt, Toby got rattled all over again. "I swear to God, Rosie, I used to pay good money at the Clover Theatre to see women walking around in outfits like that," he said.

Jerry came down the stairs and said, "It hardly covers her, if you'll pardon the expression, twat." Rosalie just sighed. "I tell you, Tobe, next year they'll all be walking around topless. There's no mystery left any more."

"The lack of mystery has never proved any deterrent in keeping you from buying the first copy of *Playboy* off the presses every month," Rosalie said.

Jerry just ignored her and steered Toby over to the bar they had set up on the kitchen counter. "This guy I know named Dicky Barrow was up in New York last week," he said, "and he saw this regular movie, where you just walked into a theater and saw it all, you know"—and he patted his chest with both hands. "Would you believe bare tit, nipple and all?" Toby whistled.

"You'll be in the first row with your bag of popcorn and your Jujyfruits as soon as it gets to Baltimore," Rosalie said.

"Ahh," said Jerry, opening the ice trays, "they'll never let that stuff out of New York. The Supreme Court will crack down on that. Beer, right, Tobe?"

"Yeah."

"Beer's all right for professional athletes to drink," Jerry explained to Rosalie, "because they can piss it right out of them. It goes right through them."

"I wish the athletes who just watch the games on TV could handle that maneuver as well," Rosalie said.

Jerry handed her a tall bourbon. "That's typical," he said to Toby. "Women are so pushy now. There's even this one now down at Laurel who wants to become a real jockey. Would you believe that?"

Toby whistled in polite amazement again.

"Listen, Toby," Rosalie said, "she's probably just lonely and is looking for a way to get around a few men. It's football season, isn't it? I tell you, Toby, you've heard of the generation gap and the racial division, but there's one worse than that in the United States they never talk about—the sex split."

"Well, Baby Cakes, then it's getting better, because it used to be a whole battle of the sexes," Jerry said.

"Yeah, but correct me if I'm wrong, Major: in a battle, you are always in contact with the enemy."

"Roger," Toby said.

"At least there was a chance at settlement then, when we were in touch. In the sex split, men and women just drift further and further apart the longer the season wears on. There's no babies born in Baltimore in July or August any more, Toby —that's nine months after the height of the season. They take the beds out of the maternity wards and use them for roller rinks."

"Ahh, come on," Jerry said, "be serious."

"Oh, really, I am," Rosalie said. "Cohabitation between the sexes, between the lawfully wed, is simply going out of style during the season. In the whole history of all the species in all the world, this is the first time this has ever happened, and it's upsetting the whole routine of nature."

"Come on, Baby Cakes," Jerry said, and he poured himself a bourbon too and ushered Rosalie and Toby into the living room.

"It's like this miniskirt," Rosalie said.

"What is?" Toby asked.

"Well, always before when the fall came, and a bunch of designers in Paris said it was time to wear something else, well, we all went out and bought it. I know you don't believe this, Jerry, but all the young girls in New York are wearing these things, even shorter than mine. Of course, you're right too, because nobody in their right minds should be wearing these things—I mean, the truth of the matter is, you really do freeze your twat off. But there's some innate sexual instinct that's telling women that the only chance we have to remain as competition for The Football is to get more and more daring and sexy. It's our only hope.

"You see, the mistake everybody is making is thinking that the miniskirt is some kind of fashion trend. That's where they go wrong. This isn't fashion. This is survival gear." She took a long pull on her bourbon and lit a cigarette. "I mean, suppose there was some other species, bluejays or ocelots or something, and all of a sudden the females were done up real strange. Well, all the naturalists would say, Hey, something's happening to the species, because all the girl bluejays are green all of a sudden, and the girl ocelots are freezing to death without any fur."

"Oh, Rosalie, you're crazy," Jerry said.

"The hell I am. You just wait till the next time those fashion designers try to make us wear real long dresses—and it will happen soon, because fashions are cyclical. For the first time in history, we'll reject those fashions—because the big fashion line comes out in the fall, in football season. It's bad enough now, but we wouldn't even have a prayer in long dresses."

"Okay, Baby Cakes, then if you extend this theory, you've got to say that pretty soon women will have to stop wearing clothes altogether, right?"

"No, Jerry, because this isn't theory, this is stark reality, and there are limits to reality, even to miniskirts. I mean, obviously, after a while everybody will be wearing them, and they will lose what power they originally had."

"Then what?" Toby asked.

"Then you guys really start to catch hell. That's when the game starts to get rough. The miniskirts are like a last desperate signal, the best semaphore we have. They say, Hey, look at us, remember us, don't neglect us for The Football. But if you don't heed the signal, we'll have to stop pleading and start attacking you."

"What, are you going to hit us or shoot us?" Toby asked, chuckling.

"Don't be so smug, Major Geyser," Rosalie snapped back at him. "I haven't seen you so cocky since you were so positive they were going to give you a football scholarship to Notre Dame."

"Ohh, that's mean, Rosie."

"Well, don't make fun of me, Toby. Mary Beth was telling me about this thing in New York called the women's equality movement. Ever hear of it?"

"Penis Envy, Incorporated," said Toby.

"A bunch of bull dikes running around," said Jerry.

"Okay, honey, I'll give you the benefit of the doubt and say that's got some truth in it. Just for the sake of argument—but that's the best argument I've got. What The Football is doing is turning us all into dikes, psychological dikes. You see, before, no matter how badly you mistreated us, at least, at least, you had to come home, and even with the cooking and the sewing and all that, we got you to ourselves, and pretty much on our terms.

"But all of a sudden, with The Football, the whole precarious balance is thrown out of whack. For four, five, six months a year, it's pro football, pro football, pro football. The wives are ignored—and not just sex; I mean unless they want to sell their souls and learn all that jargon, they're nonpeople. They don't exist. It isn't like a silly bowling night once a week or that receptionist with the big boobs that you go mooning after—it's a total thing, and all through society. Always before, you men kept us under control, because—well, you know, that old joke about nobody could win the battle of the sexes because there was too much fraternizing with the enemy.

"But now, for the first time, you are giving us great chunks of time—months of it—to think and plan by ourselves. When the miniskirts go, when dresses really do start to go down, look out for the real insurrection, because that means that at last the girlies are joining the dikes."

"Rosie, I'm sorry, but you're not cut out to write science fiction," Toby said. "Tell me about the receptionist with the big boobs instead."

"That's Jerry's department," Rosalie said, and to accommodate her, Jerry cupped his hands around his chest and jiggled them up and down, in the best imitation he could manage on short notice of Chickie's bust. Rosalie shook her head. "Oh, it doesn't do any good to warn you, anyhow, because all you men are just digging a deeper hole every year. The season gets longer. Now, all of a sudden, Jerry and all the other clowns have to start going to those exhibition games in the middle of the summer. And I can see it coming. It won't be long before they start televising games at night during the week. They'll probably start televising games from Canada soon. The Football will take over Christmas Day itself, Christmas Eve—you watch. They'll make that Super Bowl two out of three or eleven out of twenty and play the finals July Fourth."

"Rosie, I didn't know you could get so worked up."

"Oh no, I'm perfectly rational, Toby. You can see it all coming, if you just open your eyes. It's not going to be free love or wife-swapping that's going to kill the family, it's going to be pro football. I tell you, as much as I hate LBJ, at least he doesn't seem to be a pro football nut. The law of averages is that sooner or later—probably sooner—we're going to get some screwball football fan in the White House, and the hot line from the Kremlin will be ringing off the hook or a hundred thousand people will be marching on Washington, something like that, and he won't even care because he'll be watching some game."

"Oh, come on, Baby Cakes, you're really going off the deep end now."

"You just watch. Because after something like that it won't be long before the women take over. You're signing your death warrants with pro football."

Jerry put his index finger to his head and made a circular motion, chuckling derisively. "You laugh," said Rosalie, draining her drink in a final quick swoop. "I don't know whether the world will end with a whimper or a bang, but anyway, on a Sunday afternoon for sure."

16

The Tight I Formation

Johnny and Gay Tucker arrived first. "Tobe, you old sonofa-bitch," Johnny cried. "How're they hanging?" Then came Paul and Doreen Haversack, followed by the O'Reilly brothers, Timmy and Sean, and their wives, Karen and Mary Pat. Roger and Ginny Marr were next. "Tobe, you old sonofabitch," Roger cried. "How're they hanging?" Right after them, Frank and Glenda Fiola arrived. Glenda was expecting again, and everyone assured her that she appeared "radiant." Reds Ritchie and the Tatlers were late, but Young Skippy Benton showed with some stock tips, and Ted Porter, who had recently been divorced, arrived with Eileen Something. "Tobe, you old sonof-abitch," Ted cried. "How're they hanging?" As each pair of newcomers entered, Jerry would take them aside and caution them that there were a couple of niggers coming over, and not to say spook or jigaboo, or even colored, if you could possibly help it.

The party did become somewhat subdued immediately after the Tatlers arrived, but things picked back up again soon enough, when Eileen Something launched into her second rum and Bitter Lemon. She proved to be even more of a diversion than Rosalie's red corduroy miniskirt, which only Cynthia Tatler had any kind words for. "I bought one just like yours a couple of weeks ago when I was seeing my family in New York," she told Rosalie, "but Sandy won't let me wear it out of the house." Cynthia thought of Tyrone Dancer to herself, and smiled. "He won't even let me wear it in the house."

"Your husband must be an outstanding pro football fan," Rosalie said sweetly.

Toby broke away from the group that had clustered about him and made him talk about old times and the Colts. He took Sandy affectionately by the elbow and steered him into the kitchen, by the bar. They were alone there. Ginger Toogood had come into Toby's room earlier in the afternoon, just before he left for practice, and suggested that he try to get close to Sandy and to gain his confidence.

"So you see," Toby said, "between you and me and the lamppost, they just assigned me to the Guard as a formality, so I could get based in Baltimore and play for the Colts. I couldn't tell you last night at the Armory, but don't worry, I'm not going to get on your ass." Sandy nodded. "When the season is over, we'll get together some night and have a couple of drinks and dinner and work up some kind of official report just to keep everybody happy. Okay?"

"I thought it was something like that," Sandy said, and he was reassured, if not altogether convinced. Anyway, he was so delighted to be alone with a real Colt that he launched into a tedious recitation of his pro football views that lasted interminably, or at least until Eileen Something, searching for "a little freshener," came into the kitchen and asked Sandy to make her another rum and Bitter Lemon. She would have asked Toby, but she thought that Sandy was the help.

Cynthia suffered no such embarrassments. Rosalie, a concerned hostess, had made it a point to try to put her at ease, but she had then found much in common with Cynthia, and they remained in an animated conversation on the sofa that extended far beyond the limits of mere courtesy. "Well, wait, just let me show you," Rosalie said, and she sprang up and crossed to the desk in the corner. Jerry leveled Roger Marr with a withering look when he heard him whisper to Johnny Tucker, "Christ, it hardly covers her twat."

Rosalie took a large collection of papers from the desk and brought them back and spread them on Cynthia's lap. "I've been working on this all fall," Rosalie said. "Here, this is the cover." There were ink drawings Rosalie had made of skulls and crossbones and of cattle skeletons in the desert. In large letters on top, Rosalie had printed out the title:

THE AMERICAN WIFE'S PRO FOOTBALL SURVIVAL HANDBOOK

"I'm going to change 'wife' to 'woman' for the final draft," Rosalie said. "This is a battle for the whole sex."

"Right on," Cynthia said. She had just picked that up from Tyrone, and, in fact, it was the first time Rosalie had ever heard the expression, so it didn't even register with her.

"Understand, Cynthia, this isn't one of those cutesy-poo little guidebooks that helps a wife understand football so she can share it with her husband—"

"I'm tired of sharing my husband with pro football," Cynthia broke in. "That's the whole point."

"Exactly," Rosalie said. "This is not for the bleeding-heart women who are willing to be co-opted by pro football. This is for the revolutionaries among us, the brave new woman. Here, take a look at some of what I've done."

In Part One, the chapters were "Know the Enemy," "Living with an Addict," "Compromise Is Defeat," "How to Capture

Public Opinion" (write your congressman, threaten boycott of other network programs, picket stadiums, hold parking-lot sit-down strikes), "Sunday Sabotage," and "Guerrilla Warfare." These last two chapters included tips on how to screw up television reception, how to hide hubby's lucky clothes and souvenirs, how to trap him with unexpected game-day visits from in-laws, and even more devious subterfuge. Rosalie, for instance, wrote that wives should pretend to make mysterious phone calls to nonexistent lovers at a voice level just loud enough to distract a disbelieving husband from full attention to a key third-down play. And she wrote:

> Pretend to take a real interest in the game, and sit down and watch in respectful silence until you have successfully infiltrated the TV room.
> Sooner or later the husband will depart the room to get a beer or to visit the bathroom. When he returns, say something like, "I didn't know Atlanta was any good." He will say that they are not any good. Then you say, "Well, that's funny, because the announcer just said they are beating Green Bay by two touchdowns." Or, when he asks if anything happened while he was away, you say, "Nothing except they had to take out the really good player, what's-his-name, on a stretcher."

"This is dynamite," Cynthia said.

"Part Two is even more personal," Rosalie said. It included chapters on: "Saving Your Sons," "The Half-Time Striptease," "When to Withhold Your Body in Season," "Momma Don't Allow No Pro Football Spoken 'Round Here," and the finale, "Autumn Adultery: Alternative or Right?"

"What do you really think?" Cynthia asked, tapping the title of the last chapter.

"I view it a lot like civil disobedience against unjust laws," Rosalie said.

"I never thought of it quite in those terms before."

"It's a very complex, subtle issue," Rosalie went on, "and ultimately it may be moot anyway, because if all the men are so wrapped up with pro football, who will there be left to have adultery with?"

"You don't really think it's coming to that, do you?" Cynthia asked.

"Well, I'm not normally a pessimistic type," Rosalie said, "but take a look at this graph." She flipped a few pages of the manuscript that was in Cynthia's lap. "This solid line indicates US population growth, while this dotted one projects the number of available male adulterers."

"Gee, it just sort of peters out to nowhere, doesn't it?" Cynthia said.

"Oh, there'll always be a few candidates," Rosalie replied, "but as you can see by the graph, by the late nineteen-seventies they will be in such short supply during the football season as to make it sort of useless to go around looking for them."

"The law of diminishing returns, so to speak," Cynthia said.

"Yes," said Rosalie. "If my figures are basically correct, you really better strike while the iron is hot."

"Your work has sort of a doomsday element to it."

"I'm afraid so, Cynthia. Here, take a closer look at it," Rosalie said. "I've got to pass out some hors d'oeuvres." She moved first to the group that was clustered about Toby, now inquiring into the sex lives of the Colts. Since Sandy had just drifted away to talk stocks with Young Skippy, the specific question before Toby concerned the lengths of the peckers of certain of the black Colts. Luckily for Toby, he was able to sidestep the question, because just at that point Rosalie came by, passing the pigs-in-a-blanket.

Then she carried the plate over to Sandy and the others who had gathered about Young Skippy. After all, he was something of a celebrity himself, especially since Jerry always introduced him as "the Cut 'N' Run magnate," and everybody in attendance except Toby and Eileen Something had become rich young lords buying Cut 'N' Run. Along with Young Skippy and Sandy, Timmy O'Reilly and Paul Haversack, who were also stockbrokers, soon struck up a Simulated Stock-Market Conversation. A Simulated Stock-Market Conversation was, in those rocket-stock years, conducted just like a Simulated Pro Football Conversation, only, of course, virtually nobody ever lost.

Paul said, "I understand aluminums are ready to crest."

Timmy said, "I got a tip on Eberline at 10, hung with it till 26, came back in at 23, and bailed out again at the top when it hit 66."

Young Skippy said, "Telex Energy Leasing has all the earmarks of being another National Student Marketing."

Sandy said, "New York says Dynaelectron has a lot more ride."

Timmy said, "Put and call Spacerays."

Young Skippy said, "Siboney has played out."

Paul said, "I'll still take Bunker Ramo."

Sandy said, "Computer Diode."

Timmy said, "Digital Applications."

Young Skippy said, "Digitronics."

Roger Marr, walking by, said, "Electro Nucleonics."

Paul said, "Sensitron."

Sandy said, "Silicon Transis—" But he stopped dead before he could finish and stared open-mouthed across the room. The front door had opened, and he could not believe his eyes. Standing there was this monster, a huge furry beast. It appeared to be a six-foot raccoon. Everybody saw it in nearly the same instant, and gasps rent the air. The creature, raised up on its hind legs, took one step inside and then quickly flashed a sign from out behind its back. The sign said: HI! I'M RICKY, THE DON'T-LITTER-MARYLAND'S-BEAUTIFUL-HIGHWAYS RACCOON!

Then everybody just roared. "Hey, it's not a real big raccoon. It's just somebody dressed up like one," Johnny Tucker said.

The raccoon lurched across the room and threw a hug around Toby. "Tobe, you old sonofabitch," it cried. "How're they hanging?"

Toby screamed, "It's Ritchie. I knew it."

And it was. Ricky, the Don't-Litter-Maryland's-Beautiful-Highways Raccoon, reached up and took off its head, and there was old Reds Ritchie himself. "Virginia Gentleman on the rocks for the raccoon," he said, and the place broke up. Jerry ran in and handed Reds his bourbon, and everybody at the party gathered about excitedly to find out what the hell Reds was doing as a raccoon. He was always the hit of any party, but this was his best ever.

"I got to get out of this sonofabitch," he said. "It's a hundred and ninety degrees in here." Everyone laughed so hard at that, that drinks were spilled and cigarette ashes fell on the rug. Reds zipped himself partway down the front. "Look out, Glenda, I've only got a jockstrap on," he said, and there was more laughter, even more still when it was not a jockstrap at all, but Reds' famous yellow and red bathing suit that came down to his knees.

Toby said, "Where the hell did you ever get this?"

"All right, big shot, let me tell you," Reds said, and he held up his hands to make sure he had full attention. "You think you can come back to Baltimore after ten years and be the big-ass star all over again. Well, just let me tell you, old Reds is going to be the real show at the game Saturday."

"Come on, where'd you get it, Reds?" Jerry asked.

"That's what I'm telling you," Reds said. "Hasn't anybody got a cigarette? Would you believe a raccoon doesn't have any pockets?" Everybody roared again, and four people offered smokes. Reds took a light and went on. "Get this. I'm down in

Annapolis today, trying to sell a big group policy to the state employees, and I'm talking to this guy from the State Parks and Fisheries or some damn thing, and this other guy comes in carrying this outfit. They just ordered the sonofabitch. You know, it's like their Smokey the Bear.

"And so he says he can't find anybody on the state payroll crazy enough to wear the damn thing. So I said, 'Wear the thing where?' And he said, 'We're gonna introduce Ricky, the Don't-Litter-Maryland's-Beautiful-Highways Raccoon, at the Colts game this Saturday.' And I said, 'Well, what does the raccoon do?' And the guy says, 'All he does is come out before the game and carry his sign and run around and remind people not to throw their crap out on the road, and then at half time, when Santa Claus comes in for his special visit straight from the North Pole, the raccoon gets in his sleigh and rides around with him, and then if the Colts score a touchdown, he gets up and runs around some more and jumps up and down like you would expect a raccoon to do if he were a Colts fan.'

"And so I said, 'Can you see out of the thing?' And he says, 'Sure you can.' And I says, 'Can the guy who gets in him stay on the sidelines and see the whole game?' And he says, 'Sure, that's exactly what we want.' You see, they want Ricky, the Don't-Litter-Maryland's-Beautiful-Highways Raccoon right out there where all the goddamn litterbugs have got to see him. And not only that, but they're going to pay whoever does it fifty bucks. And I said, 'You mean, all I have to do is run around a little and ride with Santa Claus, and for that I get fifty and a chance to see the game of the century right on the sidelines?'

"And he says, 'That's right.' And I says—you know what I said?"

"What'd you say?" Johnny Tucker cried. With each exchange in the account, Reds had carried his audience to a higher pitch of enthusiasm. Even Sandy and Cynthia, standing almost behind Reds, at the edge of the crowd, were laughing gaily. Now, on top of the whole act, there was going to be a genuine punch line as well. "Yeah, yeah, Reds," they cried, and, "What, what?" And Reds said, "So, I said—"

And in a flash it occurred to Toby exactly what Reds had said, and what he was surely going to say again, and so he kicked him and cleared his throat and grimaced, but Reds was too worked up by now even to appreciate that Toby was trying to tell him something, and he rolled right on.

"So I said—hey, get this—I rolled my eyes, and I said, 'Mistuh, I is jest the coon you is lookin' fo'.'" And Reds bellowed in the eerie silence. It put something of a damper on the proceedings. Suddenly everybody started remembering that it was only a Wednesday. "Just a weak one, Jerry," Paul Haversack said. "It's a school night."

17

Look-In

Luckily, Halfback came into the house at that point and started barking at the raccoon, and even more of a backfire was created when Eileen Something had another rum and Bitter Lemon and decided that she would like to get into the suit with Reds. Still, none of this could dispel the embarrassing damage already done. Besides, Reds just kept apologizing, until at last Sandy could not put up with it any longer, and he snuck downstairs to the club cellar. Jerry had often told him about his collection of Colt memorabilia, and Sandy was anxious to study it.

Sandy spotted it as soon as he came down the stairs. There was the regulation Colt helmet that Jerry had once won as a door prize at a Colt Stampede luncheon, and next to it the Lenny Lyles–Ordelle Braase autographed football. They drew Sandy to them. Quiet as a mouse, he tiptoed over to the shelf, put on the helmet, and picked up the ball. Then he studied the many other wonders. There was a kicking tee once used by a rugged old extra-point man named Bert Rechichar, and a discarded cleat from one of Johnny Unitas's shoes that Jerry had bribed an equipment subaltern to let him have one day up at pre-season camp. There was also a whole array of Colt-decal souvenirs: a beer mug, a small flashlight, a lighter, a pen-and-pencil set, and several ashtrays. Finally, there were a smartly fringed pillow, a garter done up in Colt colors, a large glossy photograph of Jerry flanked by Mr. and Mrs. Art Donovan—he a former Colt great whom Jerry had once met at a crab feast in Brooklandville—and the special recording of the last minutes of the famous overtime game in New York that brought the Colts their first championship in 1958. That was also the first year that Sandy had his season tickets, so it was an especially memorable season for him.

The record, in a red-white-and-blue cover, complete with a picture of the team on one side and photographs of the "voices" of the Colts on the other, was propped up on the shelf next to Jerry's Colt license plate and the Colt beer stein where he put all his ticket stubs. Gingerly, Sandy reached up and took down the record. He tucked the ball under his arm and fondled the record, kindling the moments that it celebrated. Just being in the midst of all these tender relics was transporting him back in time. Besides, he knew the record by heart and didn't require a phonograph to hear it.

The Colts were driving for the touchdown that would bring them their first title, and Sandy could see Unitas crossing everybody up and going for the surprise sideline pass on second down. In fact, Sandy pumped the ball once himself, and heard the words on that record, long since emblazoned into his mind. "Touch—no," the announcer said. "Mutscheller took it out of bounds on the one-yard line."

Sandy moved to the center of the room, where Rosalie did her exercises, as if he were coming out of the huddle. This was it. "Barking out the signals," he heard the announcer say, and he pantomimed a call. He took the snap from center and turned to hand off the Lenny Lyles–Ordelle Braase autographed ball. "Unitas gives to Ameche," he heard the announcer say in his mind's ear. "The Colts are the World Champions! Ameche scores!" And then, as Sandy started to lope off the field to escape the frenzied crowd that was already descending toward him, he realized that he really was hearing voices.

He froze. It was not the announcer from 1958 he heard, but whispers from the bathroom right now. He tiptoed back to the special Colt shelf, replaced the ball and the helmet, and hustled over to the foot of the stairs, where he could eavesdrop in safety, in a position for a quick escape. When he had heard enough, he scurried back up the stairs. He kept an eye out, and he was not mistaken. Rosalie soon emerged at the cellar door, and, after a decent interval, Toby came up too.

Tyrone was lying down, reading a magazine on the sofa, when Cynthia and Sandy arrived back at their house. He had on a pair of Sandy's pajamas, and for a robe he wore Sandy's National Guard field jacket, complete with his colonel's insignia. Nothing gave the man who blew up National Guard armories more of a vicarious thrill than wearing the uniform of a National Guard commander. The pajamas were a little tight on Tyrone, especially across the shoulders, for he was a somewhat bigger man than Sandy. He was a bit taller too, and lighter-colored, the shade of honey.

Tyrone's good looks were marred only by a pair of curiously small ears, which, nonetheless, had never disturbed his vanity until one day when he was shown a pilfered FBI report about him, which specified that his petite ears were a "special identifying characteristic." Tyrone grew self-conscious about his ears after that, and he began to let his hair grow out and over them. He was a leader of such charm and authority that many of the people around him began to copy his style. Tyrone kept quiet, and the long hair became known as "the Afro" instead of "the small ears." Cynthia Tatler was one of only three people in the world whom Tyrone had told that story to. But then, by now he had told her just about everything he knew, because every time he would get an urge to make a pass at her, which was regularly, he would start telling secrets instead, as one way to divert himself.

Cynthia and Tyrone being alone together all day long was not at all a healthy arrangement. As a matter of fact, Tyrone was going bananas, and at an accelerated pace since one afternoon early in November when he had chanced upon Cynthia coming nude out of the bathroom. That afternoon he promptly told her where the United Afro-American Alliance had cached all its weapons, the names of all peace officers in the United States who would tip the UA-AA off, and where every important black revolutionary was hidden, the Third World over. Then Tyrone started in on bank accounts, and, that done, on special phone numbers. Even then, he had to go lock himself in his room and read National Guard mortar manuals. The brief sight of the undressed Cynthia stayed clear in his mind. She was tall and thin, with wonderfully sporty little pop-up breasts and a gorgeous fine face, but she was even better nude than he had imagined. This was because Cynthia was one of those rare women with absolutely erotic bones. This is not to say that the other things about her did not periodically occur to Tyrone, but with the bones as well, he was going berserk.

Twice in November his contact had it virtually set to hustle Tyrone out of the country, but he vetoed the escapade both times at the eleventh hour, because he was determined to depart only when Sandy was away from the house. He could not be a tacky guest and make a play for Cynthia beforehand, but he certainly did not want to leave the Tatler residence without at least giving Cynthia his best shot.

He watched her now, as she came into the house, home from the Starts' party, and went and stood by the mantel. Cynthia flipped her coat over one shoulder and leaned there, slinky, every beautiful bone leaving an impression against her clothes and driving Tyrone battier. "Well," she said, "the baby-sitter certainly looks comfortable."

"The baby-sitter is fine, thank you very much," Tyrone answered. "And so is the baby. Not a word out of him."

Sandy was still outside, trying to get the huge Oldsmobile from Mickey Shadducks Olds into his one-car garage that was made for Falcons. Cynthia picked a lipstick off the mantel and rolled it idly in one hand, while she pleasantly asked Tyrone how he had amused himself while they were at the party. "Oh, you know," he said. "Read a little, watched a little television, blah, blah, blah."

"Oh? You must be losing your touch," Cynthia said sharply. Tryone looked up in surprise at her tone, and she flipped him the lipstick. "If you could sneak a girl in here, I would expect you to think of better things to do."

He sat up stiffly and brushed his hair back nervously over his ears. "Please don't tell him, Cyn. It was just this one time."

Cynthia put a finger to her lips and nodded. She liked to believe that this was only a personal matter between herself and Tyrone, because Cynthia had come to take a great delight in being the most important person in the world to a person who was so important. She had determined that the situation was rather like a black *Casablanca*. And don't be naïve: it wasn't by any mistake that Cynthia came out of the bathroom that time without any clothes on while Tyrone was just standing there. As long as she had Tyrone in the house, she wanted to play him off against Sandy. Unfortunately, the more Cynthia worked to make her husband jealous, the longer the season lasted and the less he cared about anything except the Colts.

Now Sandy burst into the house and took the center of the room, barely able to contain himself. "Have I got something to tell," he said.

"What's this?" said Cynthia.

"I saved it from the party to tell you both," Sandy said. He still had his overcoat on. "About an hour ago I went downstairs to the club cellar. Jerry's got this fantastic collection of Colt souvenirs. But what do you think I found down there?"

"Take off your coat," said Cynthia.

"A Ku Klux Klan Klavern," Tyrone suggested.

"No, come on." He ignored both answers. "I found Toby Geyser down there in the lavatory with none other than Mrs. Rosalie Start."

"Rosalie?" said Cynthia.

"The lavatory?" said Tryone.

"Yeah. How 'bout this? They're playing a little house together. She's going to meet him tomorrow night at eight at Parton's."

"What's Parton's?" asked Cynthia.

"Oh, it's just an old farm out on the Joppa Road where the white kids go to park," Sandy said.

"Having a little information like that on that cat can't hurt," Tyrone said.

"That's right," Sandy said. "He tells me he's just in Baltimore to play for the Colts, but as long as you're in this house, Ty, I don't like him snooping around."

"Well, this is your lucky night, my man," Tyrone said. "I was in touch with my contact tonight."

"Contact." Cynthia snickered.

"It won't be long before I'm leaving. We got the passport set, the schedule, the plans, blah, blah, blah. It looks real good, thank you very much." Then he stood up and reached out to the Scrabble board on the coffee table. The letters were strewn all about. He and Cynthia played a lot every day. He took some letters and rearranged them. "Here, my man, I make my move." He turned the board around on the Lazy Susan until it faced Sandy. Cynthia came over from the mantel and looked down too. The letters spelled: CUBA.

"And I'm going out of here first class too, thank you very much," Tyrone went on, taking the floor. "All the scuffling and hustling we were doing to get me out of here on banana boats and in secret compartments—no, my man."

"How?" Sandy asked.

"I've had a lot of time to think, all cooped up here, and I really got to figuring. Now, this is the most powerful nation on the face of the earth in the whole history of the world, but you take all our defenses"—Tyrone said the word with the accent on the first syllable, as football coaches have taught us to—"all the bomber planes, all the early-warning systems, all those big-ass missiles stuck out there in North Dakota, blah, blah, blah, but what good are they if the cats in charge aren't paying any attention, all at once. Now, when might that be?"

Sandy said, "You mean like when, what hour in the day?"

"No, my man, in the year, in the whole year."

"I get it," Cynthia cried. "Christmas."

"Shoot, Christmas," Tyrone said, shaking his head. "That's for kiddies and reindeer, and ain't none of them handling the missiles in North Dakota. No, it's just any old pro football Sunday."

"Hey, you're right," Sandy said.

"Thank you very much. That was my mistake when I tried to blow up that last armory in California. I thought I was so cool, making my move at three in the morning. But that's nineteenth-century thinking; that went out with high-button shoes.

If I'd waited a few days till the Rams played the Forty-Niners, I could have blowed up every armory in the state in broad daylight. Shoot, on Super Bowl Sunday you could play a number on the head of any building in this country—airports, national monuments, Fort Knox, whatnot. Or take 'em over. If I was the Russians or the Chinee, I wouldn't listen to no old-time generals talking about weather reports and troop movements and all that old who-shot-John. I'd just say, We head in on the opening kickoff, thank you very much.

"So you see, if you could take the whole country over during the Super Bowl, well, I sure as hell can sneak out of Baltimore when the Colts are playing in a MUST game. I'll just stride onto that three-o'clock plane for Puerto Rico, and nobody will even look at me. If J. Edgar himself was taking tickets, he'd just ask me if I knew the score. My contact says this is so good it's going to change the whole revolutionary business. No more of this banging around, operating under cloak of darkness. You just wait till it's a key third-down play. You could walk away with the Liberty Bell itself if the Eagles ever got improved enough to get in a big game again. I'm just going to dance right out of here, thank you very much."

"It sounds absolutely perfect, Ty," Cynthia said.

"Well, nothing's ever perfect," Tyrone said. "But I do believe now that with just a little help from God and one other white man, this will be foolproof."

18

Sacking the Passer

The next day was Thursday, only two days before the big game, and the coach came up to Toby at the start of practice and told him that he was going to use him primarily to run kickoffs back. "And don't worry," he said, "I'll get you in on some plays too."

"Don't change anything around on my account," Toby said.

"No," the coach said. "Using you on kickoffs is a natural. It'll be less wear on Lenny Moore. And I really think it's to our advantage to put you in for some plays. The first two-three times you go in, the place will be up for grabs. Even the Packers have got to be diverted. So we'll put you out on the flank as a decoy a couple times, and they might even double-team you just to be sure. Then, just when they think you're only in there as window dressing, then we'll really get Johnny U to chuck it to you. Okay?"

"Yeah, sounds good," Toby said, and, in fact, it did.

Memorial Stadium was stark and bare this Thursday, only two days before the big game, and even though it was a mild, windless afternoon, Toby felt chilly in the big place and kept his windbreaker zippered over his sweatshirt. He tried not to look over toward the press corps, standing up and down the sidelines like sentinels. Their demands upon him had lessened somewhat as the week wore along, but he was still as much of a continuing story as the MUST game itself.

The coach noticed that Toby reacted toward the press's presence, and he put a reassuring hand on his sleeve. "Don't let any of those reporters near you till after practice. Some sonofabitch from a magazine called up this morning and wanted to know if he could sleep in the same room with you the night before the game. He wants to do a goddamn twenty-four-hour diary on you, like the day Lincoln was shot." He pounded his clipboard. "Look, Geyser, you've had to take an unbelievable amount of shit so far, and I appreciate it that you haven't bothered me about it."

"Hell, I've been the nuisance for you," Toby said.

"No way. Would you believe: I'd start you if you had just one more week. I watched you close the last couple days. You got your legs. That's all I needed to know. You still got your legs. I saw you once when I was scouting you at Army. I saw you run a kick back against Utah State. You didn't have a block on the field. You broke three tackles and zigzagged through the other eight guys."

Toby smiled. "Yeah, that was a mother."

"You coming okay with the plays?" Three photographers and one TV crew ran out to photograph Toby and the coach walking along.

"I got a pretty good concept of the basics."

"I figured you could get enough this fast. Now the rest of the way, just concentrate on the 30-angle series, right and left. That's what we'll probably call if you're at setback. And when you're on the flank, Johnny knows we'll only split you off the double wing. Nothing fancy."

"I feel like I got it," Toby said. "I do."

The coach slapped him on the back. "Okay, alternate in the first backfield taking handoffs from Johnny, and then I'll have Michaels kick off to you." Toby nodded, cut past the photographers, and loped away at a good pace. He did feel limber and really part of things for the first time. The players had started calling him Audie Murphy, which he liked, for he knew it meant a teasing kind of acceptance. For the first time, too, he was really catching Unitas's rhythm on handoffs, and now the balls were not slapping into his belly, as the cliché always suggests, but they were nestling in there neatly, the perfect give-and-take, no need for slapping and grabbing.

The pass patterns were coming to him too, so that he could run them without thinking, concentrating everything on the feints and the catch. He snared one on a flat-out dive, and even the usually deadpan Unitas grinned and called, "Nice catch," loud enough for several writers to hear it and devote entire columns to the incident the next day. By the time Toby went back to the goal line to shag some kickoffs from Lou Michaels, Toby was really lost in the game for the first time. He could even visualize the Packers bearing down on him as he took the kicks and burst up the field, and was so totally immersed in the sport of it for the first time that he was not even aware that the coach had come over to see him.

"Hold it, Toby," he said. "Take a break. I've got someone to introduce you to." Toby looked up to find a big, burly, mournful man standing by the coach. He was wrapped in a blue Colt cape, but Toby did not recognize him as part of the staff. The stranger, his eyes avoiding Toby's, suddenly threw out his hand and said, "I owe you an apology, Major." It was a curious thing for anyone to say, and the way he blurted it out, it was obvious that he had it on his mind to say it. In fact, he was so intent on saying it that he had forgotten to exchange greetings first.

"Toby, this is Bruno Barrett," the coach said, and Toby said

hi, trying to remember who Bruno Barrett was. He knew that
he remembered the name vaguely from somewhere.

"Nice to meet you," the big man said at last.

"What do you mean, an apology?" Toby asked, and he sank
his hands into the top of his pants.

"I scouted you in high school."

"Bruno's an assistant for Notre Dame; one of the all-time
greats," the coach said, and then Toby remembered the name.
As a kid, he had absolutely lusted to go to Notre Dame. He
wasn't Catholic, but Notre Dame had always had the best teams
when he was growing up, and he had become a devoted fan of
the Irish. By his junior year at Towson, when Toby was already
a high-school All-American, his desire to attend Notre Dame
had become complete. Several top Notre Dame alumni personally visited him, including Jim Mutscheller, who played
tight end for the Colts, and Bob Williams, the great Irish
quarterback, who had grown up only a few miles from Toby.
After that, no other college even interested him.

There were intense pressures too. Alumni from the University
of Maryland beseeched him to matriculate there and single-
handedly restore the Terps to gridiron glory. Toby's marks were
good enough so that all the Ivy League schools promised him
admission; and Navy and Army, of course, and sixty-four other
schools from almost every state of the nation. He was that good
a prospect. Several well-known football factories made una-
bashed illegal offers, and one Western institution researched his
life so completely that the coach not only promised Toby a car
and a fake job that would pay $600 a month, as well as the
usual scholarship, but also assured him that when Rosalie graduated in two more years she would be guaranteed a full scholarship herself, spending money, a complete wardrobe, and the
Campus Queen title. Another coach, then the most successful
one in the South, a well-known teetotaling Baptist lay reader,

called up Toby one night when he was drunk and shacked up with an airlines stewardess, and not only offered him the pick of campus coeds if he would just come and visit the school, but even offered the same deal to Reds Ritchie just because he happened to be at Toby's house at the time and answered the phone.

Nothing, however, could dissuade Toby from his singular dream of going to Notre Dame and leading the Irish to a national championship. By the time he was a senior, the most acclaimed high-school player in the country, he saw no reason why this could not all happen. Toby didn't even bother to apply to any other school but Notre Dame.

"It's on my conscience ten years," Bruno Barrett said, and in such anguish that Toby was as sorry for him as he was curious. "They should have fired me."

"Why, Mr. Barrett?"

The big man drew a heavy breath. "Because I'm the one that advised Notre Dame not to give you a scholarship. That's why."

Toby blinked at this confession. "My God," he said. "Then you changed my entire life."

Bruno fought not to cry. "I'm sorry. I had to get this off my chest. I've lived with this."

"It's okay," Toby said. "There's no sense crying over spilt milk, sir."

"I come to scout you your senior year," Bruno said, determined to talk now. "Every report we had on you was out of this world. And you played real fine that afternoon I saw you, too. I remember. You was all over the field."

"Then why'd you turn me down?" Toby asked, and the coach drew closer too.

"God as my witness, Toby," Bruno Barrett said, "I've played that game back in my mind a million times, and I know I must have been wrong—you proved that—but I still think I did the right thing. I don't know what it was, but you looked scared of contact. You were flashy-like, but you weren't competitive. No heart, forgive me."

Toby looked at Bruno square on. "Just tell me one thing," he said. "Do you remember which game it was, sir? Just tell me that."

"Like I said, I never forgot that game," Bruno replied somewhat indignantly.

"It was the Bel Air game, wasn't it?" Toby asked.

"Howdja know?"

Toby shrugged and pulled a hand out of his waistband and patted the old scout on the shoulder. "You were right that day, Mr. Barrett. You're a helluva scout if you had the guts to turn me down that day."

Tears welled in Bruno's eyes, until at last he had to duck his head and shuffle his feet. "I seen you play a half-dozen times at Army, and you were never the same," he said. "There, you always come to play all heart."

"You were absolutely right that time, Mr. Barrett," Toby said, and he shook the old man's hand and backed away.

The coach took Bruno by the arm and led him off. "God bless you, son," he called, sniffling. "You're a credit to the game."

Toby signaled to Lou Michaels to resume kicking and moved back just inside the end zone to take his place. The first kick was a good one, and even in the still air it stayed high, coming down almost softly, it seemed. Toby moved over a few steps to catch it, but as he watched, his concentration left him, and it was not really the ball he saw coming toward him.

Everyone has seen so many movies by now that people are able only to remember in movie flashbacks. Just as in all the movies, something in the present begins to fade out, and beyond it, in a dissolve, something in the past appears. Thus, as the ball off Lou Michaels' educated toe came tumbling gently toward Toby, it slowly began to disappear before his eyes, and instead it was replaced by Rosalie walking down the stairs at her house toward him in a haze of crinolines under the new sea-green formal with the huge organza bow that she had bought expressly for the Senior Halloween Dance that night.

19

Down and Out

She drew closer and closer, until he could reach out and hand her the magnificent wrist corsage that he had just purchased at Radebaugh's Florist. In all his life, before or since, Toby had never seen anything so beautiful as Rosalie walking down the stairs to greet him that night. It made the rustle of her crinolines seem like the Melachrino Strings playing an LP in the background. He was so overcome that not only did he completely forget about the big game against Bel Air next day, but as soon as he reached the wheel of his father's orange-and-yellow De Soto, he impetuously withdrew his high-school ring and thrust it at her. Toby had meant to wait until after the dance before at last bestowing this turquoise delight, but he just could not contain himself. Rosalie, sobbing with joy, ran back inside her house to obtain some adhesive tape to wrap around the back of the ring so that it would fit her finger.

Naturally, everyone at the dance noticed right away. For the girls, it meant that Rosalie and Toby were now engaged to be engaged. For the boys, it meant that Rosalie would have a

nice token to remember her erstwhile virginity by. In fact, this
was not too far from what was on Toby's mind. Compatible as
he and Rosalie were at endurance feeling and dry-humping,
Toby was getting worried that the service-station rubbers that
he carried in the back of his wallet—with, figuratively, Rosalie's
initials on them—would wilt and decay before he was ever able
to put them to use. The vaunted high-school ring, he was sure,
would be the key that unfastened the Mojud hose from her
garter belt and peeled off the panties beyond.

When the band picked up the tempo for "Wake Up, Little
Suzie" for the fourth time, Toby begged off. "Come on," he
said. "I can't stay up too late. That's a really big game tomorrow."

She clutched his hand, and they moved quickly through the
crowd of well-wishers that parted obsequiously for them. "Get
'em tomorrow," everyone said, and a few members of the dance
committee threw paper leis around both their necks. "Hawaiian
Holiday" was the motif of the dance. Some of the gang were
hanging around the big papier mâché pineapple, cadging cigarettes at the entrance to the gym. "Take it easy, Tobe," Frank
Fiola said.

"Any way he can get it," Reds Ritchie hooted.

"Eat it on a stick, you bird dogs," Toby replied, and he
hustled Rosalie along to the car. "Want to get a hamburger or
something at Murray's?" he asked, as he was obliged to. Murray's was the favorite drive-in everybody hung at, only then it
wasn't called a drive-in but a milk bar.

"No, I'm really not hungry," Rosalie replied, reading from
her part. Silence followed, and they walked on a few more
steps in deeper thought.

"Well, let's go over to Parton's and talk awhile," Toby suggested suavely and nonchalantly, as if the idea had just occurred to him.

"Sure, okay," Rosalie said, tucking her sea-green formal and all the crinolines safely into the front seat. Casually, Toby slipped his hard-on into the creases of his rented tuxedo, set the car on automatic pilot, turned on the car radio, and punched around for a good song. This meant that he had one hand on the steering wheel, one hand on the radio buttons, and one hand draped around Rosalie's shoulder. It was not easy, but then, everybody did it. Toby was in luck too, for WCAO was playing one of his favorites.

"We start 'em, others chart 'em," the DJ said. "Now let's rock with 'School Days' by the merry Mr. Chuck Berry!"

"This one is really moving up fast on the Silver Dollar Survey," Toby said.

"Hitbound," said Rosalie. The electric guitars set up their beat in prelude to Mr. Berry's vocal rendition.

"It's got a great beat, doesn't it?"

"You can really dance to it," Rosalie agreed.

"What I like best about it," Toby said, "is that the song tells a real story, about the kids going to school and then out to dance and everything. People are always saying that teenagers' music is silly and stupid, but they just don't ever listen to the words."

"People are always out to get teens," Rosalie said. "Nobody ever writes anything good about teens."

"Yeah, and there's all kind of kids who work in hospitals and safety patrols and in Civil Defense and everything."

Rosalie didn't have any more observations to offer on that subject, so Toby tried to mine another conversational vein. He wanted to really talk to Rosalie before he put the make on her, so that God would know for sure that he viewed her as a nice girl. "Do you think 'School Days' will become a standard?"

"Gee, I don't know. I don't know how they make standards."

"I think the award-winning DJs get to vote," Toby suggested, but Rosalie didn't have anything more to say about that either. She was too intent on studying her prize, his ring.

"You sometimes just wonder what it was like before rock-and-roll," Toby said, not only at his nostalgic best but seriously concerned with the state of the world in those sad bygone days. Many teeners worried just so about that. Toby put the subject out of his mind, though, when he turned into Parton's. It was a deserted old riding academy that had failed years before, and the present owners cared nothing for the place but were merely hanging onto it until the land could be rezoned more profitably. (A high-rise apartment is there now, as a matter of fact.) The cops would come around once a year or so, make a big stink, and confiscate a lot of beer, but outside of that annual display of token vigilance, they were content just to let the kids from Towson have the place to themselves.

"Well," Rosalie said after a while, "in the old days, I think there were a lot more standards."

"Yeah, there was more close dancing then," Toby said, as he cut the De Soto across the open space that had once been the riding ring and down one of the paths that led to the stables. They had their spot staked out there, and in one neat motion he put on the brake, turned off the lights and the ignition, and, turning to Rosalie, kissed her madly. Pausing then only for an obligatory expression of love, to assure her (and, once again, God) that this was no mere cheap physical attraction, he put the feel on her with the second kiss and started to try and unzip her with the third one.

This particular evening, what with Rosalie in her complicated sea-green formal with the huge organza bow, Toby had to defer to her for some assistance, an operation which was not helped materially by either her wrist corsage or the Hawaiian leis. In fact, it took so long for them to clear away the impediments to her breasts that, by the time they did, the car was getting cold, and Toby had to start up the engine to heat it again.

Of course, this diversionary action did provide him with the opportunity to attempt furtively to unzip his fly. That maneuver never came off too smoothly, mostly because, even under the best of field conditions, it is impossible to unzip a fly sitting down with one hand. It cannot be done. He managed it this time with his usual élan, while lodging Rosalie supine on the seat, with her head propped comfortably up on the door handle. Then he made the customary entreaties—guaranteeing no diminution of respect—but, even with the ring in her possession, Rosalie held firm and would not be tinkered with.

So, as passion began to overwhelm Toby's interest in debate, he at last thrust his lonely member into that forest of crinolines in the general area where he presumed her crotch to be. Her crinolines, which were never intended for this role, crinkled and cracked around the line of scrimmage. Toby, propping himself up off the floor with one hand, hung there for a while until he regained his breath, then swung back up on top of her and started in again. This time it took quite a bit longer, and he had to pump hard and purposefully. It was not, either, that he desperately wanted to go again, but it was just that he had made a warm spot for himself in that swarm of crinolines, and besides, wedging himself and Rosalie into exactly the proper positions was such a task that it simply seemed inefficient to go through all that for the sake of just one dry hump.

It proved to be an agonizing mistake. By the time Toby had dropped Rosalie off at her house and limped and dragged up the steps to his own room, he was in mortal pain. He was to remember these moments years later, when the shrapnel tore into him, for it comforted him then to know that his body could withstand so much greater pain. At home, he sat on his bed and gingerly removed his rented tuxedo pants, revealing a slab of a thing that peeked out the fly of his drawers. It was slashed and bloody, full of gashes the whole length; but then it was also all shriveled up, as if to best protect itself from any new assaults. The crinolines had not even spared Toby his balls, raising welts on them. Chunks of pubic hair had also been ripped loose. Even Bingo Turf, yet undiscovered, could never possibly wreak such havoc. It hurt so much, Toby couldn't even put on his pajamas. He tried to go to sleep sitting up on the toilet.

At her house, Rosalie was in a comparable state of mental anguish. She spent upward of an hour in the bathroom trying to scrub the blood off the crinolines and what had reached through to her panties. It was clear to her that, despite all her efforts—more than any one of a thousand good girls would manage—her maidenhead had been cut asunder. She tossed fitfully in her bed, hearing the foghorns of New York harbor as her honeymoon ship pulled out to Bermuda and she tried to explain to her bridegroom (who suddenly appeared to be wearing a clerical collar) that it was not at all as he imagined, that annulment would only burden her with more unjust shame.

At his house, Toby at last stirred himself from the toilet seat, took two aspirins, and coated his dick with Ben-Gay. Then he locked his door and tried most unsuccessfully to sleep on his back in the cold room without any covering.

The next afternoon, in a toilet stall in the locker room, Toby carefully selected three skin-colored Band-Aids of various shapes and sizes and applied them as effectively as he could to the most damaged areas. This was hard, for there were almost no undamaged areas to put the sticky ends onto. With somewhat more success, for vanity's sake, he was able to darken in the bare spots where the crinolines had pulled his hair out, with his mother's eyebrow pencil. Finally, he packed his privates, like good china on a trip, jamming in as much cotton as his jock-strap could hold, carefully hoisting it up and on, biting his tongue all the while to keep from screaming.

He stumbled onto the field for warm-ups running like a duck on ice, and Bruno Barrett, settled into his seat on the fifty-yard line, had to check his program three times and ask several people in the vicinity before he was convinced that Number 22 really was Toby Geyser, the brilliant, graceful All-American, who could run a hole through the wind. At last, after the kick-off, having given the kid every possible benefit of the doubt, Bruno took out his note pad, shook his head, and jotted down: "Moves Akwardly [sic] ? ! ! ?"

If Bruno had also been scouting cheerleaders, he would have surely given low marks to Rosalie too. She was not moving around at all with her usual abandon and did no jumping or leg-splitting whatsoever. Her pleated little white-and-purple skirt hardly ruffled in the afternoon breezes, except occasionally when she put herself full into the cheers that demanded only a lot of arm-waving and shouting:

> Florida oranges, Texas cactus,
> We play Bel Air just for practice!
> Go, Generals, go! Yeahhhh!

Rosalie's actions were based on her conclusions, arrived at after deep thought, that the events of the previous evening were simply not sufficient to have broken her maidenhead. She decided that they had probably only jarred it loose a little, and with judicious exercise she could nurse it back to its full self. She was aware that broken bones often knitted stronger than the originals and was certain that, virtue being its own reward, her maidenhead would eventually be held to her insides with the strength of veritable grappling hooks. Of course this was not an easy conclusion to reach, for Rosalie, like all her contemporaries, had been carefully schooled in the understanding that 24.6 million American teenage good girls had had their maidenheads torn to pieces riding horses, on the saddle horns. Everybody knew that, or, a yway, that 24.6 million bridegrooms on the boat to Bermuda accepted this explanation without serious argument. Nevertheless, Rosalie did not want to take the easy way out and join the 24.6 million other saddle-horn claimants. Instead, she undertook her own brand of therapy, moving in teensy-weensy little baby steps and jumping not at all.

Naturally, all the other cheerleaders and all the students in the cheering section looked on knowingly, absolutely convinced that she had really done some screwing for Toby for that ring. Jerry heard about it from some guys on the bench in the third quarter and dropped a pass watching her instead of the ball.

Toby himself was in too much pain to even consider Rosalie. It even hurt him to try to lean over and put his hands on his knees in preparation for the pass from center. Bruno noticed immediately that all the other well-drilled Generals backs came perfectly to this basic position. "Sloppy!!" he wrote down, clucking his tongue. On the first two plays from scrimmage, Toby called for his fullback to carry the ball, but with third and five he knew he could postpone his moment of truth no longer. He called for himself, a tailback end sweep.

He thought he could feel the octagonal Band-Aid peeling loose just before the center pass, and he reared up. The referee threw a penalty flag for illegal motion, but it was too late. The pass-back from the center was on its way, and Toby took it and loped to the outside. The blocking was good. A linebacker loomed before him, but this was Jerry's end, and he took him out cleanly with a solid block. Toby could see that if he cut back to the inside there were yards of daylight ahead, but instead he opted to take the first down and to just run the ball out of bounds, unmolested. Bruno frowned, baffled. "The kid has no instincts," he said out loud, in disgust. Toby was in a panic to reach the sidelines, but just as he did, the Bel Air safety man caught him. The peak of his helmet dug into Toby's thigh, then swung over and scraped his maimed area. The safety man was only a mouse of a fellow, and his tackle wasn't even a hard one, but Toby just caved in on the spot, a foot short of the first down. Bel Air turned down the penalty, and Towson had to punt.

Bruno cursed. "NO GUTS! ! ! !" he wrote, and, till he grew tired of it, he underlined that phrase over and over as the game wore on.

Actually, Towson won easily, and, except for the practiced eye of an expert like Bruno Barrett, Toby appeared to be his usual spectacular self. He broke loose on two touchdown runs of 53 and 37 yards, he passed for over 200 yards (passing didn't hurt so much), one a picture-book 72-yard TD toss to Jerry, and he completely screwed up the detailed Bel Air scouting report by letting the other backs handle the ball so often. Nonetheless, Bruno could see that Toby was basically a fraud. The report he filed on Toby is still on record at South Bend, and although no one dares call it to Bruno's attention, sometimes the other coaches and scouts take it out and read it over, just to marvel at how Bruno could have missed so badly. It reads:

> This boy is an honor student, a leader on and off the field, and though he is a heathen, he is a Class A youngster. He is naturally talented, with all the basic qualities I was assured that he possessed. He has an outstanding arm, great open-field speed, and is a brilliant signal-caller. He plays tailback in the single-wing, and could make either a T-quarterback or halfback for us. BUT, he is *not* OKOP [our kind of people]. He has no guts, he has sloppy habits and bad instincts.

He always runs to the outside and will do anything to avoid getting hit. He is a high-school hero, but he would be a college zero. No heart! ! ! ! If we gave him a scholarship, he has so much natural ability that he would be sure to make the team, but he could not play regularly for us, and since he comes with such a hot-shot reputation, I'm sure that he would sulk and be bad for the Irish team. Scholarship recommendation: a big NO! !

Three months later, on a Friday in February, Toby got a form letter informing him that, unfortunately, Notre Dame's scholar-athlete quota was filled, and he could not be offered any financial assistance there. For the first time in years, he went up to his room and cried. Then he picked the only two pimples he had, on his neck, washed his face, and went off to pick up Rosalie. She knew something was wrong, but not until they reached their spot at Parton's did he tell her. She tried to console him then, and suddenly found great faults in Notre Dame, but he remained distraught. He drank almost all of a six-pack of beers that he had swiped from home, and grew even giddier from smoking eight of her cigarettes. Toby never smoked. He pulled himself up from dry-humping her and told her then, as he tucked himself in, "So I've decided, Rosie. I'm going to Army."

"No, Toby, not the Army."

"Army, West Point," he snapped. "If Notre Dame doesn't want me, I'll never make the pros anyway."

"Toby, a soldier, that's not you," Rosalie cried, snuggling up against him.

"The President's a soldier, for Chrissake," he said. "If it's good enough for the President, and it's good enough for Pete Dawkins, it's good enough for me. Somebody's got to stop the Communists from taking over the world."

It was, of course, never ever the same again, although they

kept up appearances until he graduated. They just played out the routine. Rosalie kept hoping she could change his mind, somehow: North Carolina, Maryland, Princeton, Penn State; she tried a new college on him every time. Besides, she didn't want to break up with Toby and start dry-humping with somebody else, inasmuch as that would stamp her to be a slut.

Their last date was the Senior Prom, the night of graduation, when he was in a rented tuxedo .nd she in her crinolines again. When he caught sight of them, Toby lost the urge even to go through the motions, and then he didn't even seem to care when Rosalie said that, since he was heading off to Plebe camp, she thought it best that both of them "play the field." Toby assured her that he would always respect her, and she handed him back his Towson ring, suggesting that they "stay good friends always" as she peeled off the adhesive tape. Then, since they had nothing else to do or talk about, Toby started up the car, they left Parton's, drove to Murray's, and finally had that hamburger.

20

The Tacklers Converge

Although it had been almost a decade since he had last seen it, Parton's looked the same as ever to Toby. Even the welcome mat, an ancient NO TRESPASSING sign, still hung on grimly by one nail, flourished by the same familiar old initials and obscenities. He eased his rented car along until the road opened up into the abandoned horse ring, and only there, for the first time, did the place seem changed. This was because Parton's was empty of vehicles, except for one lonely car parked way down at the other end. Back in the old days, before teenagers had conquered hypocrisy, the place was always jam-packed with heavy neckers, even in a blizzard or on religious holidays or exam nights.

Toby could tell that the other car there was not Rosalie's station wagon, so he steered away from it, parking so that he could watch for her. She was not late, either, for the only difficulty she had in getting away from the house had been in obtaining a baby-sitter on a week night. She knew that Jerry would get home late anyway, because, providently, Pine Brothers and Moore had rented a hotel ballroom for its employees and clients to celebrate with a "Pack in the Pack" party that evening.

In point of fact, Jerry was already bent out of shape by the time Rosalie left the house. Not only was the MUST game two days away, but Reds Ritchie had promised Jerry that he would make his inaugural public appearance at the party as Ricky, the Don't-Litter-Maryland's-Beautiful-Highways Raccoon! It was all so electric that after Jerry had had his fifth (or eighth) bourbon and water he became more sexually alert than he had been in months, since the week in September when the Colts had routed lowly New Orleans so completely that there had not even remained the usual crying need to prepare material for that week's Simulated Conversations. Now, at the party, Jerry decided that Chickie could simply no longer contain the mad desire that she possessed for his lean, lithe body. At last, when he was on his way to the men's room, she led him on brazenly by going to get her coat. "Oh, hi, Jer," she cooed, putting on her casual act, as if he meant nothing to her. Jerry winked and handed in his coat check too.

At Parton's, Rosalie parked her station wagon a discreet distance away from Toby's car (for no good reason, really), and then scurried across the field toward him like a fugitive. He flopped over into the back seat and opened the door for her.

They both said, "Hi," and fell into a real movie embrace. Nobody was playing any games. To encourage expedition, Rosalie hadn't even worn any underwear. "Hey, I feel like a real piece of ass," she said gaily, unzipping her dress down the back.

"Oh, great." Toby sighed. "Thanks for that."

"Don't be so sensitive, Baby Cakes. This is really and truly tit for tat. You're my piece of ass too."

Toby, displaying a certain amount of courtliness, if only to occupy himself, took off his coat and folded it in a big bundle so that Rosalie would have a headrest. He also apologized for the accommodations. "There's just no hotel in town where I could go without being recognized, Rosie."

"Ahh, I know, the price of fame."

"Anyway, it's a big car, and I left the heat on."

"It does have a certain period flavor," she mused, shifting to give him some room beside her. "The criminal always returns to the scene of the crime."

"What crime?"

"Misdemeanor?" Rosalie suggested. "Well, psychologically, anyway, I gave in to you the last time we were here."

"What does that mean?" Toby asked, propping himself up on an elbow and looking her in the face. "Hell, that was the night you gave me my ring back."

"That was only at the end, stupid. I came prepared to present to you my whole intact body. You could have ravished me if only you'd asked. I would have even done it up right and gotten in the back seat."

"You're kidding."

"Oh, no. I was ready to trade my virtue to keep you from West Point. This is really just a raincheck."

It occurred to Toby that a man's life is supposed to flash in front of him in the instant before he faces death. He had never had that claim proved to his satisfaction in Vietnam, but now, twice in this one day, first with old Bruno Barrett, now with Rosalie, he was seeing the last ten years of a life he had never had, of Toby Geyser, civilian breadwinner, rush before his mind, as if they had been pulled out of some neglected computer bank. In the last scene, the really good one, he was sitting before a roaring fireplace with Rosalie and their kids and the English sheepdog, drinking hot chocolate and telling them about the day's Dow-Jones averages. He kept that in his mind as he rattled kisses over her body, since it lent an air of legitimacy to the proceedings.

"At last," Rosalie whispered, "my lamb chop, my hero, my raincheck." And they began to entwine, at least up to the limits of entwining prescribed by back-seat design. But even that modified entwining was nearly complete, and he could just feel his lips on hers, when suddenly her head jerked away from his and more or less disappeared. The reason was that the car door had opened.

Toby looked up and found himself staring into the business end of a very nasty little pistol. There was an explosion of light, and he was surprised, if not necessarily relieved, to find himself still alive when it was gone. He blinked and looked out past the gun and finally was able to make out the figure of the man who was holding it. His bushy head was framed by the moon, and Toby recognized him immediately. "Oh, no," he said.

"Move over and give me room," Tyrone Dancer replied.

Sandy was just arriving home from the "Pack in the Pack" party. "Ty's gone," Cynthia said at the door.

Sandy stood dead in his tracks, waves of sobriety sweeping over him. "He doesn't leave until Saturday," he said.

"That's what I mean, honey. He took my car and went out."

"Oh my God, your car," Sandy cried. "All they have to do is catch him in your car, and we're dead. Where is he?"

Cynthia drew a deep breath. "He's gone after Toby Geyser. I'm sure. He heard you say last night that he'd be with Rosalie Start at that Parton's place."

Sandy slammed his gloves to the floor. "Damn it. They probably got half the Secret Service tailing Geyser." He started out the door and back down the front steps.

"Sandy, he's got the gun," Cynthia screamed in a whisper, remembering the neighbors.

"Oh, no," Sandy said, but then he jumped into the car anyway, turned it around, and headed off in the direction of Parton's.

Jerry was gratified to discover that Chickie was as circumspect as she was ravishing. He liked that in a woman. Though crazed for him, she gave no public indication whatsoever at the coat-check counter of her true feelings. Indeed, such was her consideration for his reputation that she would not even tarry down in the parking lot, lest prying eyes see them together there. Jerry had to rush to his Mustang and really peel out after her. She headed north up Charles Street, and it was not until they reached the hill going up toward Mount Vernon Square that Jerry was able to get in close enough range to blink his lights to assure her that he was still behind her. So determined was Chickie not to let on to cagy observers that she was his mistress, however, that she continued to pretend not to take note of his signals.

In fact, Chickie was so discreet that she got too far ahead of Jerry, and when a big oil truck pulled out in front of him at the stoplight by the Greater Baltimore Medical Center near Towson, he simply was unable to run the light. By the time he could start up again and round the bend, Chickie's car had disappeared. Obviously, he understood that she had pulled off somewhere by the side of the road to wait for him, but somehow their signals got crossed and he could never catch sight of her again.

He sighed at this patch of bad luck, but smiled at the thought of other magic evenings ahead that he could permit Chickie to share with him. It also occurred to Jerry at this point that he was still desperate to take a leak. He had forgotten all about that in the excitement. True romance will do that to you. Luckily, however, he knew just the spot nearby, so he turned onto Joppa Road and cut over to Parton's, where he had often gone before to unzip his fly and unburden himself.

21

An Exchange of Punts

"Come on, move over," Tyrone said, waving his pistol.

Rosalie just sighed. She was quite aware of the fact that she was lying spread-eagled and virtually buck naked before some crazy black man with a gun, and she figured that if there was any chance for survival it lay in agreement—and politely. She did not even really comprehend when she heard the man say, "Come on, get up and cover up," because, of course, that was the last thing that she expected a killer-rapist to say.

"Just don't hurt her," Toby said.

"Believe me, I don't want to, Mr. Touchdown."

He waved the pistol in their faces, though, to emphasize his options, and Rosalie felt obliged to raise her hand and ask permission. "Is it all right with you if I cover this, please?" Her left breast, the one nearest to Tyrone, was still hanging out completely.

"I regret to say, yes," he said, and then, pointing the gun in the general direction of Toby, he added, "And in the interest of propriety, please tuck that away too." Sheepishly Toby straightened himself out and zipped up his fly.

Tyrone leaned back against the door almost casually, although he kept the pistol pointed in the right direction. "I'm sorry to have interrupted at such an inopportune time, but I have a proposition to make." He paused and chuckled devilishly. "Ahh, the night is rife with propositions."

"Who is this?" Rosalie asked.

"Tyrone Dancer," Toby said. "You know, the militant."

"God, I hate that word," Tyrone said. "It hangs on me like a burr. I feel like the tiny sheikdom of oil-rich Kuwait."

Rosalie squirmed. Her dress had not been pulled all the way down in back, so her bare ass was resting on the vinyl, and that itches something terrible. "What do you want, Dancer?" Toby asked.

"Ahh, of course—what do I want? What I want, my man, is to do my best to make sure that Colt fans and war fans will never learn the awful truth, that Mr. Touchdown USA was balling in the back seat with his best friend's beautiful wife."

"Cut the crap for the captive audience," Toby snapped.

"For, my gracious, that disclosure might help destroy the credibility of our noble war effort. It might even upset the point spread. And not to mention what they would be saying about Mrs. Start around the Towson Plaza."

"Quit it, Dancer."

Tyrone leaned back smugly and waved the pistol around for a little effect until he had to lower it out of sight as a brace of new headlights came down the road. All three watched tensely, but the car turned and headed in the other direction, parking over next to where Tyrone had left Cynthia Tatler's Mercury. Its lights went out, and Tyrone picked up again. "You know, Mrs. Start, the real question—"

"Since you know me so intimately, you can call me Rosalie."

She was changing her tone, beginning to think that rape and/or death might be a much easier price to pay.

"Well, now, that is neighborly, Rosalie. I'm Tyrone, or Ty, if you wish." He bowed. "And now, Rosalie, as I was saying, the question before this august assembly is: exactly what would you estimate is the value of your public reputation as an honored wife and mother?"

"Do you mean, how much would I pay you to keep this little hanky-panky a secret?"

"Precisely!" Tyrone crowed. "Only I'm hesitant to accept 'hanky-panky' as a fair assessment of what would be more accurately labeled adultery on the open market, or simply fornication in more visceral company."

"Tyrone," Rosalie said, "I usually don't argue with a man with a gun, but just to set the record straight, be advised that you crashed the party a moment too soon to really catch us, uh—"

"In the act?" Tyrone suggested helpfully.

"In the act."

"For God's sake, Rosie, do we have to go into details?"

"All right, then," Tyrone offered, in the spirit of conciliation, "how would you plead to the charge of attempted balling?"

"Guilty to the lesser charge."

"Rosie, please."

"Well," Tyrone said, "no need to fuss. We can settle this by taking a look at the instant replay." He reached down onto the floor at his feet and picked up the camera. Rosalie gurgled with a disgusted surprise; her eyes had been closed in bliss when the flash went off. Toby had forgotten all about it in the excitement. "It's a Polaroid Swinger," Tyrone apologized. "It was all I could get on short notice."

"It isn't the usual blackmailer's fare, is it?" Rosalie asked.

"No, but then I am vamping at this. Has anybody got a

watch? We have to wait thirty seconds for the picture." Unfortunately, no one had worn a watch, and the automobile clock was, of course, broken, even though the car had only 736 miles on it. So Tyrone had to count: ". . . a thousand and twenty-eight, a thousand and twenty-nine, a thousand and thirty—and one, two, three to grow on." He pulled back the case and slid the new picture off, then cracked the door to activate the overhead light. He scrutinized it carefully."It's a little blurry around the edges, but—"

"For Chrissake," Toby said, "it's not going in a contest."

"Oh, God," was all Rosalie could say. In the picture, Toby was looking up, his mouth open in slack surprise, his face framed stupidly between her two bare breasts. Both their faces were easily identifiable, and for that matter, Rosalie thought, so were her breasts. It was the first time that they had ever been photographed, and it helped confirm her opinion that they bore a marked resemblance to Toni Winston's in *Playboy*. Rosalie was the sort who looked for silver linings.

"That's a damn good Polaroid, thank you very much," Tyrone said, quite proud of himself as the artist. He closed the door and slipped both the picture and the negative into his pocket. "All right, my friends."

"I have the feeling, Toby," Rosalie said, "that now we're finally going to get screwed."

"Oh, Rosalie," Toby cried, and Tyrone shrieked in delight.

"Since we appear to be in the spirit of things, I think it's time we began serious negotiations," he said.

"Order in the court, the monkey wants to speak, all the little alligators take the back seat," Rosalie said.

Tyrone glared at her but went on without comment, "Now, Rosalie, a few weeks ago you sold a hundred shares of Cut 'N' Run through a broker in Richmond, didn't you?"

She gasped, confirming the fact. "How did you know?"

"Never mind, if we play that game, how did I know you were here? I've got my sources, and one of my sources says that that little sale means that something like twenty thousand plus is just sitting in your savings account. Right?"

"You know," she said. He was dead right except for the $1500 she had withdrawn to go shopping in New York. But then, she really hadn't even told Jerry about that.

"Tomorrow I want you to draw out ten thousand of that."

"In cash?" asked Toby.

"Greenback dollar bills. You got it, my man. You tell 'em that money is for Mr. Touchdown, and don't worry, nobody in Baltimore is going to question it. You tell 'em it's for war bonds, you tell 'em it's for betting on the game. You tell 'em it's for fixing the game. I don't care."

"Okay," Rosalie said.

"And one other thing. Aside from that hundred shares you sold, you still got a lot more Cut 'N' Run sitting around in your name. I'm not greedy. I just want one other hundred-certificate signed over to me. That will provide me a little nest egg for those days when I have become only an aging onetime militant. There are no real pension benefits in this line of work." He sat back, satisfied, and even seemed a little disappointed when neither Rosalie nor Toby appeared to be as pleased with the arrangements as he was.

"Look, I know it's expensive," he hastened to add, trying to smooth things over, "but giving up a little Cut 'N' Run is certainly better than having this on the six-o'clock news." He patted the picture in his coat.

"Please," Rosalie said evenly. "Go easy on the melodrama."

"And we get the picture and the negative as soon as you get the money?" Toby asked.

"You get everything this side of S & H Green Stamps, my man. Look, I'm no blackmailer. I'm just trading in a little over-the-counter, thank you very much. Everybody's a broker now-adays. I'm just another broker in a bull market."

Rosalie nodded in resignation. "Can he zip me up in back?"

"Yes, indeed. It's time for you to go home anyway. Mr. Touchdown and I have some logistical matters to discuss. So say night-night." He climbed out, affording them a bit of privacy.

"Sorry, foiled again," Toby said, pulling up her zipper.

"Oh well, I guess it's just not in the cards for me to be a piece of ass. But what the hell, I could never play badminton either." She turned around and pecked him on the cheek. "See you later, alligator."

"After a while, crocodile," said Toby.

Tyrone was standing by the door when she slid out. "I am sorry," he told her.

"Well, you certainly ought to be," Rosalie said. "If you're gonna blackmail people, you ought to at least be proficient enough to let them get their money's worth first. I mean, really, as a consumer, that's not asking a whole lot."

Tyrone bowed his head and kicked at the dirt with his feet. "You're right. I can't argue with constructive criticism."

"I ought to turn you in to the Better Business Bureau," Rosalie called over her shoulder, stomping away. She was still in such a fury when she drove off that she didn't even notice that the Mustang she passed, parked by the side of the entrance road, was her husband's.

22

Suicide Squad

Luckily for Rosalie, Jerry was trudging off into the woods to wee-wee when her station wagon passed by, so he didn't see her. On the other hand, Sandy came into Parton's only a minute or so later in search of Tyrone, but by then Jerry had located himself, with a good vantage, behind a scrawny bush. Besides, if there was one car in Baltimore that Jerry was familiar with, it was Sandy's flashy 1968 Oldsmobile from Mickey Shadducks Olds. Jerry was really intimate with Oldsmobiles.

This was because he had to sit right next to Mickey Shadducks himself in Section 10 during every Colt game, and as soon as there was time out on the field, Jerry would encourage Mickey to start talking about electric carburetors and reusable trunk space and other inside automotive expertise. This was the closest thing to commercials at the stadium for Jerry, and it made him feel more at home.

Mickey liked to talk about Oldsmobiles, too. Many of his best friends called him "Mr. Oldsmobile," and his wife, Cheryl, was herself a former Olds mechanic and a crack Demolition Derby Drivette. Jerry would start off a time out by saying such things as, "Mickey, is the roadability of an Oldsmobile affected by the engine deposits in the alternator?" Or, "Mickey, what does it mean when the little red light on the far side of the dashboard goes on?" Mickey could and would answer any such questions, and, as a result, Jerry became an authority himself on Oldsmobiles and therefore recognized Sandy's as soon as it came into Parton's.

He was so flabbergasted when he saw it that, even though he had hardly set about his business, he zipped himself up and came scurrying out to his Mustang. He started the car, but kept his lights out, using the moon to sneak up on the Olds. As a consequence, he was almost on top of it before he realized that the car parked right next to Sandy's was none other than Chickie's. This called for some fast fancy thinking.

Now, ever since Jerry had made a fortune off Cut 'N' Run and become a man of leisure, he sometimes took days off or left the office early. On these occasions, especially during the off-season, Jerry would watch the game shows on TV. Unfortunately, a dangerous trend had manifested itself on many of the shows, and it had seriously affected Jerry's thought processes.

What had happened was that these shows had been overrun by celebrities—notably Soupy Sales and Rose Marie—and these big names had been given all the real brainwork to do. Previously, save for a few mystery guests, ordinary people who wrote in for tickets in advance were permitted to do the bulk of the participating. Now, though, the celebrities had taken over and reduced the regular people to drones. For example, if the moderator asked what country was directly south of Detroit, Michigan—Mexico, Canada, Luxembourg, or Nepal?—the celebrity was the one who would answer the question, while the everyday housewife was required only to decide whether the celebrity was right or wrong. For instance, Wally Cox would answer, "I'll say Canada," and the homemaker would just push her buzzer and say, "No, I believe Wally is wrong."

As a consequence of this new TV policy, huge numbers of Americans had, like Jerry, forgotten how to think for themselves. They needed celebrities to think for them. It was like with the flashbacks in the movies, where everyone had forgotten how to go about remembering otherwise. In Jerry's case, his mind had deteriorated to the point where he could no longer even buy or sell a simple stock without first listening to the views of his favorite celebrities. These were Jan Murray, Nanette Fabray, and good ol' Charlie Weaver. Jerry once spent a whole afternoon hearing Jan out on the subject of whether it was necessary to have a Diners Club card and an American Express card both, or if not, then which one.

Now, with similar large puzzlers set before him at Parton's, Jerry required a whole lot of thinking done, so he not only had Jan and Nanette and Charlie crowd together in the back seat of the Mustang, but he also got his favorite moderator, the genial and bespectacled Bill Cullen, to sit with him up front and conduct the proceedings.

"Let's think about what Chickie is doing here first," Bill Cullen said.

"Okay, I'll call on Jan Murray to answer this one," Jerry said.

Jan answered, with a leer, that it was obvious that Chickie had come to Parton's because she knew that Jerry would follow her there, and it was an ideal romantic spot to make beautiful music together. Jerry quickly rang his bell and said that he agreed wholeheartedly with that reply.

"Next, on the subject of why Sandy is here at Parton's, we'll turn to the distaff point of view, and the ever-lovely Nanette Fabray," Bill Cullen said. "Hi, Nanette."

"Hi, Bill." Then Nanette went on to answer that she was sure that Sandy had noticed the passion that Chickie evinced so blatantly back at the "Pack in the Pack" party, and had tailed them to Parton's just to do a little amateur snooping. Jerry rang his bell and said that that sounded like the right answer to him.

Then, after pausing a minute for the commercial, which gave Jerry time to light a cigarette, Bill Cullen came back on and said that now it was time for Charlie Weaver to think for Jerry. Charlie warmed to the task by citing some humorous examples that related closely to this very situation, that had just been relayed to him in a letter from home from his mother. Then he thought for Jerry: "I don't agree at all with Jan and Nanette." (Jan made a face.) "I think you're the odd man out, Jerry. I think that it is Chickie and Sandy who have a thing going, and they came out here to Parton's to make it themselves. You don't even see them in their cars, do you? They're probably going to it off in the woods right this very moment."

Of course! Thanks to Charlie Weaver, Jerry saw clearly for the first time. He was so agitated that he slapped his hands together and forgot to ring his bell. All the men in Sandy's seats in Section 10 were forever speculating on what Sandy was going to use his final two season tickets for. Now, at last, it was obvious that Sandy was going to use at least one of his tickets to obtain a white woman—and if that wasn't galling enough, it was the same white woman Jerry had staked out for himself. So enraged that he forgot to take his leak again, Jerry popped out of his car and stamped off into the bushes to try to catch Chickie and Sandy red-handed.

Tyrone climbed into Toby's back seat after Rosalie sped off, and lounged against the door. "Now don't let me forget this camera when we leave," he said.

Toby, leaning away against the other door, frowned. "I have only two things to say to you, Dancer."

"Yes?"

"First, please don't point the pistol. Even if I was able to trick you, overpower you, kill you, and destroy the picture and the negative, it would be too complicated. I won't try anything."

"Cross your heart?"

"And hope to die."

Tyrone put the safety on and stuck the pistol in his waistband. He also debated letting on to Toby that there weren't any bullets in the gun anyway, but he decided to hang on to that nugget of information.

"And second?"

"The second thing, Dancer, is that I hate your fucking guts."

"My, my."

"But nothing personal, you understand. Merely circumstantial. Would you like a glass of champagne?"

"Really?"

"I got a big bottle and two glasses up front," Toby said. "You see, this really was to have been quite an occasion. No trick. Go ahead, look."

Tyrone raised up enough to see, and then motioned for Toby to retrieve them.

"Now, about hating your fucking guts."

"Shall we drink to that?" Tyrone asked.

"If you won't be self-conscious about it," Toby replied, starting to work the cork free. "You see, I have spent the better part of my mature life, the highlights of it anyway, trying to seduce Rosalie Start, *née* Totter. You cannot believe the incredible impediments that have been thrown up to thwart this honest, earthy intention. I have been thwarted in this—that's a great word, *thwart*. A thwart really sounds like a thwart."

"Thwart," said Tyrone.

"And when it comes to Rosalie, wow, have I been thwarted. In pursuit of the former Miss Totter, I have been thwarted by a very real fear of lethal underwear, by a technological revolution that seeks to improve on God's green grass, and now by a social revolution that seeks equality and justice for men of all races." Tyrone smiled self-consciously at that. "Yes, that's you—you're the agent of the latter."

Toby took out a couple of cigars and offered one to Tyrone, who accepted it gracefully. Toby lit them both and went on. "Now, all this wouldn't be so bad in one way. After all, there are thousands, millions of men the world over who spend a great deal of time trying to screw certain women, and fail, no matter how long they try. Right?"

"Absolutely."

"Wait a minute. I've almost got this cork. I'm going to roll down the window and shoot it out. Okay?"

"Go ahead."

"But the thing with me is that every time I don't screw her, it changes my life drastically. That's the unfair part. I'm the only man who keeps getting into trouble by failing to do something that all the other men get women into trouble by doing."

Tyrone nodded sympathetically on behalf of Toby's plight and watched him explode the cork out of the window.

Sandy heard the blast as he was sneaking around the periphery of the clearing toward Toby's car. Even though he had been prepared for the worst, he really could not believe that Tyrone would actually shoot Toby, and when he heard the shot he was so stunned that he just stood up and started running through the bushes toward Toby's car. He had taken only about three steps, however, when a sneak blow from behind came thundering down on the back of his head, and he crumpled unconscious to the ground.

"Hmm, imported," Tyrone said, sipping the bubbly.

"I told you, this was to be quite an occasion."

"Well, I really am sorry I had to crash your little rent-a-boudoir, my man, but time is a luxury with me now. I'm departing the Land of the Free Saturday, when everyone is occupied watching your star-spangled debut."

"Very clever," Toby said, and, to himself, he toasted Ginger Toogood for concluding so accurately that Dancer was ready to make his escape.

"That brings us to your little assignment," Tyrone said, fishing in his pocket for a piece of paper. It was an order for two first-class airplane tickets on Pan American flight 87, leaving Baltimore Friendship Airport on Saturday at 3 p.m, nonstop for San Juan, Puerto Rico. It was all carefully spelled out for Toby. "Perhaps you could guess it, my man, but a slight mid-course correction will modify our destination somewhat." He tilted his cigar at Toby. "Maybe I'll be able to send you a box of their finest."

"Your ticket is for a Sergeant Ernest Kimberly?" Toby said, reading off the sheet. "Sergeant?"

"It's a touch I added when I decided to enroll you in the caper," Tyrone explained. "Sergeant Kimberly will be a much-decorated Vietnam hero going south for some well-deserved rest and relaxation, blah, blah, blah. It's really a dandy disguise, particularly when the best-known war hero of them all personally buys the sergeant's plane ticket."

"And the other ticket is for a Miss Daisy Champion?" Toby said, reading again off his orders.

"Merely another àlias. Ideologically, of course, Cuba is a paradise, but socially, well, between you and me, participating in an agricultural revolution can get a little tedious for a healthy, fun-loving individual. It's not the sort of place you want to visit stag. I've had the pleasure of some very gorgeous company in my hiding, and if all goes well, that beautiful lady will be departing with Sergeant Kimberly, thank you very much." Tyrone raised his glass to drink to the possibility.

Sandy's head, throbbing already, would have been split clear through if he had heard that revelation. As it was, it was all he could do to drag himself to his feet and stagger off in retreat, through the bushes and back to his Oldsmobile. After only a few steps, though, he heard some distinct murmuring, and, naturally, he took up a more guarded pace. After all, somebody was around bopping him on the head.

As he drew close to the murmuring, Sandy crouched down on his knees and parted some pine branches. There, a few feet away, in the middle of an old bridle path, he saw Jerry and Chickie standing, swaying in the middle of a long kiss. Jan Murray, and not Charlie Weaver, had been right after all. Sandy shook his head, baffled. All he ever did was run into one of the Starts making time on the side with someone else. Moreover, in duplication of the club-cellar scene of the night before with Rosalie and Toby, Sandy soon heard Jerry and Chickie making plans for a more complete resumption of their activities at her place in Glen Burnie, Saturday, immediately following the Colts' game. Sandy was beginning to feel like the Starts' social secretary.

He watched until they were finally through smooching, and then, at a safe distance, followed, seeing them go back down the overgrown path toward the clearing. Soon he heard a car door slam, but he kept hidden in some bushes just off the path, taking no chances until he heard the car actually start up and leave. He was still huddled there when he heard footsteps approaching, and he froze when they stopped right next to him. Forlornly, breathlessly, he waited to be discovered and to take another clout on the head. That was when Jerry began to pee on him.

"Just enough for another glass for us both," Toby said.

"Blackmail appears to be a more urbane business than revolution," Tyrone replied, proffering his glass again.

"How did you ever get into it, anyway?" Toby asked. His cigar went out and he had to light it again.

"Oh, just sort of drifted," Tyrone said, looking dreamily out into the dark. "Actually, I started out to be a football-player."

"Didn't we all, Ty. Do we go wrong because we all start out to be football-players, or because so few of us end up that way?"

"No college would mess with me. I was ahead of my time. All the other cats were walking around saying that they were afraid of the atom bomb, and I said, No, man, the Establishment is the power that blows you up every day. That wasn't fashionable then. Too bad. I probably would have made someone a helluva halfback. I could probably even whip your All-American ass. I did a 9.5 hundred."

"No way," Toby said. "I was 9.4, 9.3 with a wind once, and I'm bigger than you, too. Besides, I think I might have made a better revolutionary than you if I hadn't been a halfback."

"Yeah, but a soldier boy. Why that?"

"Ty, it's a long, gory story, the substance of which is that I never screwed Rosalie."

"Well, you're probably lucky, my man. The trouble is not with you and me, the ones that didn't screw the girl and didn't make halfback, the trouble is with the ones who did. Those are the sonsofbitches who get in charge and spend the rest of their lives trying to make the world over like their high school. You ever notice that? The good old days are always high school.

"Listen, if some college had taken me in football, I'd probably be all-pro now, driving a big-ass car and running a restaurant in the off-season with my name on it, and if you'd ever screwed Rosalie, you'd probably be sitting before a roaring fireplace now with her and a bunch of kids and an English sheepdog, sipping hot chocolate and reading the day's Dow-Jones averages to them. And neither one of us would ever get out of high school."

Tyrone shrugged at himself. "Come on, that's enough bullshit from me," he said. "I got to show you this tree out here where I want you to leave that suitcase full of Cut 'N' Run tomorrow. Then Saturday, you just get Rosalie to come to the airport and pick up the picture and the negative, and we're all even. Right, my man?"

Toby nodded and drained the last drops into their glasses, then let the bottle fall to the floor. "Oh well," he said, "just another dead soldier." Tyrone roared in delight.

Once Jerry realized that he was standing there pissing on Sandy, and, on the advice of Nanette Fabray, stopped doing so, he helped him to his feet and back down the path to their cars. That was when, suddenly, just as they entered the clearing, Chickie jumped out of her car and ran up to them.

"Christ, Jer, they're after us," she cried, pointing down to the other end of the clearing, where two figures had just broken out of the woods and were running toward them at breakneck speed. The two runners were bearing down hard, closing ground with each stride. And they looked like they meant business.

"We gotta haul ass outa cheer," Chickie suggested, and after quickly assessing the situation neither Jerry nor Sandy felt obliged to quarrel with that analysis. All three turned heel simultaneously, scattering into the woods. Unfortunately, Sandy was hardly into the safety of the bushes before he got bopped on the head from behind again and collapsed under another bush.

Chickie caught up with Jerry shortly thereafter and begged him to protect her from the swift strangers. He pulled her down behind a tree and waited silently, ready to defend her if the intruders should come into the woods after them. He lost all concern with that possibility right after Chickie reached down and unzipped his fly.

Now, who are the strangers and why were they running at Jerry, Sandy, and Chickie? Had they done something to Toby and Tyrone? Were they, possibly, Toby and Tyrone running away from something? Or were they secret agents from DANG and DONG? Ginger Toogood herself, perhaps? And not to forget poor Sandy—while we know who tinkled on him by mistake, who kept hitting him on the head on purpose? And why, for that matter? And why did Chickie go all the way out to Parton's to unzip Jerry's fly? You can do that sort of thing almost anywhere. Was Cynthia really going to leave Sandy and take off for Cuba with Tyrone? Had pro football actually brought marriage to that pretty a pass? If so, there is just no telling what Cheryl Shadducks might do to Mickey Shadducks, is there? Was Toby ever going to make it with Rosalie? Ever? Was Cut 'N' Run liable to go up some more on the over-the-counter?

Well, many of these questions are toughies, but we can get a hunch that Cheryl Shadducks, for one, really is up to tricks, because it seems that she is wearing her crash helmet again for the first time since she retired from the Demolition Derby. And considerable light can certainly be shed on the speedy two strangers—except, perhaps, for the benefit of Sandy, who was still conked out, and Jerry and Chickie, who were otherwise occupied.

"Beatja," Toby said, pounding happily on the car hood. "I

told you not to race me." He collapsed alongside the car, smiling broadly, and Tyrone, trailing by only a couple of steps, flopped down beside him.

"I would have won if I didn't have to lug the gun," he said, breathing heavily.

"Look, uniforms were optional," Toby said. "No excuses. If you had won, you would have bragged it all over Cuba that you beat me, everybody's All-American. Now, fair and square, I expect you to send me a box of their best cigars."

"I'll include a bottle of champagne too, thank you very much," Tyrone said, and they stood up together, caught their breaths, walked into the woods, took a leak on what happened to be Sandy, got into their cars, and drove away.

23

Stunting

Saturday morning, the day of the big game itself, Toby's wake-up call at the Sheraton-Belvedere came at eight-thirty. He put back the receiver, threw off his covers, and headed off for the bathroom. "Good morning," said Ginger Toogood.

She was sitting in her raincoat at the end of the bed, and Toby couldn't immediately decide whether to be embarrassed because Ginger had caught him with a hard-on or because she had caught him with a hard-on and did not seem to be moved by it. Anyway, he sprinted the rest of the way into the bathroom and popped into the shower. "Oh, don't be a silly goose," Ginger said, following him and sitting up against the basin. "I grew up with brothers."

"Such cheek," Toby replied, coming out of the shower with a towel wrapped firmly about him. "And now you distract me at the crucial moment when I must apply Rise menthol instant push-button magic lather to my face to make my sluggish whiskers stand up like so many little tin soldiers."

"This is no time for cutesy-poo," Ginger snapped, standing right up to his face. "I've got a critical mission for you today."

Toby laughed out loud. "Listen, you poor man's Mata Hari, this is my big day. All America is watching me. I'm the cynosure of a hundred million eyes, the name on the tips of fifty million tongues, the last, best hope of the military-industrial-football complex—and you want me running around delivering some takeout orders."

Ginger breathed testily, and Toby began to wonder whether she had anything at all on under the raincoat. It was a real spy's raincoat with lots of buttons and belts, pockets and flaps, and a high collar that she had turned up against her magnificent long golden locks.

"Rise coats the skin and makes it as soft as a baby's boomy."

Ginger glowered, but for once Toby had some kind of edge on her, because the bathroom steam had fogged up her horn-rims and made it impossible for her eyes to stare right through him, as they customarily did. Toby strengthened his position then by whistling the familiar part of *La Traviata*. That is the part that goes: la laaa, la, la, la, la, la, la, la, la, laaaah, etc. Toby had found that this segment is not only perfectly operatic-sounding—no matter how it is hummed or whistled, or by whom, it has opera written all over it—but it was also the *only* bit from any opera that Toby knew, except for the toreador song from *Carmen,* and that really couldn't count as real opera, because every kid in school learned to sing, "Toreador-a, don't spit on the floor-a, use the cuspidora."

Toby had learned the bit from *La Traviata* from a barber on York Road who used to whistle it whenever he was shaping flat-tops. People would look at him, and he would say, "I'm sorry. *La Traviata.*" Toby noticed that this made a deep impression on everyone, and, at least when he wasn't around the barbershop, he began to work the same routine. Soon people came to hold Toby in great new intellectual esteem, because in America nobody knows the first thing about opera, the United Nations, barometric pressure, or wine. Anyone who appears to be knowledgeable about any one of these subjects can get away with murder.

For Toby, just whistling those few bars from *La Traviata* had obtained for him hotel, plane, and restaurant reservations, a summer job, several fancy party invitations, including a whole Fourth of July weekend at Virginia Beach, a good deal on a used car, some pussy, and a discount price on a Swiss watch. Of course Toby had learned to improve on the barber's bare-boned apologies. Toby would not just say, "I'm sorry. *La Traviata.*" He would say, "I'm sorry. The picnic scene from *La Traviata.*" Or, "I'm sorry. The magnificent flower aria from *La Traviata.*" Or sometimes, just for the hell of it, Toby would say, "I'm sorry. The supermarket scene from *La Traviata.*" Or, "I'm sorry. The tender speedboat aria from *La Traviata.*" It never mattered; Toby had learned that nobody would ever dispute anyone who seemed to know a little opera.

Ginger was taken in as much as the next fellow. She could tell right away that Toby wasn't just another clod whistling trash straight off the Top 40.

"I'm sorry," he said. "The rollicking mountain aria from *La Traviata.*"

Naturally, Ginger nodded as if she had known all along, and she immediately began to treat Toby with a new deference. "Look, I don't want to be cross, and I do appreciate how important your game is today, but I must ask you to do this. I hate to bother you, but this just came in on direct orders from DANG."

Toby stopped whistling and pointed his razor at her chest. "Aha. I thought we were never to let that word escape our lips."

"Exactly," Ginger said. "Don't you see? I made this rare exception so that you would understand the severity of this mission."

Toby whistled the same number over again. "I'm sorry. My favorite—the unforgettable candlelight scene from *La Traviata*."

Ginger looked off dreamily into the distance. She didn't know a rat's ass about opera either, except for the toreador song from *Carmen*. "Such a rich, strenuous interlude," she said.

"And with my multi-edged uranium-coated Gillette safety razor, the whiskers are removed, zap, as smoothly as a frog whisks away warts."

"Please, Major, this is a crucial assignment."

"And does it painlessly, without nicks, tears, abrasions, contusions, or pains of neuritis and neuralgia."

"Listen, all you have to do is put a bug in Sandy Tatler's office at the Fifth Regiment Armory."

Toby shook his head forcefully as he wiped off his face. "You've got the wrong boy. I can't even change a fuse."

"Oh, it's really not a bug," Ginger added quickly, chasing after him into his bedroom.

He slumped down there in a chair. "Mark my words, Ginger Toogood. At this very moment, somewhere out there, there is a child, yet a mere broth of a lad, who will someday—God willing, in our lifetime—who will someday lick shaving, make it as commonplace as an everyday heart transplant."

Ginger picked up a handsome black leather briefcase, and rapped it softly. "Look at this. Just listen to me."

"Oh, I've been listening. You want me to bug Sandy Tatler's office at the Fifth Regiment Armory. Only it's not a bug."

"That's right. It's a very sensitive, long-term tape mechanism in this briefcase. It's activated only when someone is talking. It would be recording this now, as a matter of fact."

"Hello, General," Toby said.

"Oh, you cut-up," said Ginger. "The tape can last literally for weeks. It just sits there recording. You don't have to push a button, twist a wire—nothing. Just walk into Tatler's office and hide this somewhere."

Toby shook his head emphatically. "That's not my job. I wasn't brought into this as a second-story man."

"Look, Major, this is vital if we're ever going to get Dancer. We've got a wiretap on Tatler's home phone, but we're not getting a thing on it, and it's simply too tricky, politically, to get permission for a bug at the Armory. The National Guard lobby howls if you just try to ticket some weekend warrior for double parking. Maybe Tatler's in touch with Dancer from his Armory office. He would know that that was a safe phone."

"Ginger, as usual you have pleaded your case eloquently. But —why me? You can hire spies from Manpower to hide brief-cases."

Ginger exploded with her cackle again, the one she saved for when she found Toby especially stupid. "That's the beauty of it. You're the one person no one would dare question. You just stroll into the Armory"—and Ginger flashed a couple of keys and pantomimed opening locks with them—"hide the brief-case, and go off to your game. There's a Sergeant Ansel Topper in charge of the place, but he's got fifty-yard-line seats to the game today and surely won't even be there. The whole thing won't take you more than ten minutes out of your way to the stadium."

Toby sighed in submission. "I just stick it somewhere in the office?"

Ginger beamed. "That's all. Do you know a good hiding place?"

"Absolutely. Tatler's got stacks of this stuff called Bingo Turf piled up in his office."

"What in the world is Bingo Turf?"

"Ginger, it's a long, gory story that would boggle even your mind. Just be assured that I can hide our tape recorder in the stuff."

"I knew I could count on you, Major," Ginger said, crossing briskly to her room. "You're aces."

Toby cursed when she closed the door, he hastily apologized to the tape recorder for being so common, and then he dressed and set off for his mission and the MUST game.

By the time he pulled into the players' parking lot at Memorial Stadium a short while later, Toby was satisfied that he was becoming a master in the art of leaving briefcases hidden about. He had just slipped the one containing the tape recorder into the folds of the Bingo Turf at the Armory as proficiently as, the day before, he had placed the one containing the Cut 'N' Run money and the plane tickets in the tree at Parton's. Now, it was left only for Rosalie to pick up the negative and the picture from Tyrone at the airport and settle that matter forever.

Toby stepped quickly across into the Baltimore locker room, and although it was still hardly ten-thirty, both Sandy and Jerry were already preparing to leave their houses for the stadium. They both tingled with a special excitement too, for this was to be the day that Sandy would lose Tyrone during the game, and the day that Jerry was to gain Chickie after it. At Section 10, they drifted fitfully into a Simulated Conversation with Sergeant Topper and Mickey Shadducks that lasted until Mickey started moaning about how mad his wife was at pro football. As a former Demolition Derby Drivette, Cheryl Shadducks was not the kind of wife you wanted mad at you—especially in a community-property state.

"Is the missus going to hurt you, Mickey?" Sergeant Topper asked, swilling coffee from his Thermos and pounding his clipboard to suggest a crazed Cheryl Shadducks raining down blows on Mickey. Sergeant Topper always carried coffee and a clipboard, even out of military jurisdiction, because he had learned that anyone in the service drinking coffee or holding a clipboard is excused from all tasks or responsibility.

"It's something drastic, I don't know what," poor Mickey said, uncapping a beer from his Scotch Kooler. "I haven't seen my Cheryl worse since the time I chucked the TV downstairs and killed the cat accidentally when Dee-troit scored on the desperation play in the last second."

"Ahh, it's just an annual phase the wives are going through," Jerry said. "My wife is writing some book about how wives can fight back at pro football."

"The football season is good practice for the wives for menopause," Sandy said.

"Well, I'm real worried still," Mickey went on. "She's started wearing her tailored asbestos demolition suit for the first time since she left the Derby, and she hung me in effigy in the family room the other night during the Colts' highlights show."

Mercifully for Mickey, the Colts came out for their pre-game warm-ups at this point, and all travails were forgotten in that instant. Everyone in the stadium grabbed for binoculars and zeroed in on Number 22, cheering his proficiency at jumping jacks. The stadium was only partly filled, but every eye was on Toby, watching him constantly. In the whole place, in fact, only Jerry and Sandy did not continue to devote their full attention to Toby.

Jerry was distracted regularly by a crinkly, sweaty piece of paper that he kept pulling from his pocket and sneaking fond, covert looks at. It was the paper on which Chickie had written her address: "6205 Moss Way, Glen Burnie" was all that it said, but then, it was the only concrete thing that Jerry possessed of hers, reminding him of the modest favors that she had surprised him with the other night, and of the more spectacular treats she had in store for him after the game. He had searched diligently for Moss Way on his Arrow Street Guide—Glen Burnie is a suburb south of Baltimore, near Friendship Airport—and had then carefully determined the fastest route there, as well as several alternatives.

Sandy, meanwhile, kept glancing up as compulsively as Jerry looked down. Sandy could not for long withdraw his eyes from the huge Longines-Wittnauer clock that topped the scoreboard, for it measured all his hopes. The kickoff was at 1:05, Tyrone's contact was to pick him up at 1:30, and the plane was scheduled to depart at 3:00. With any kind of luck, Sandy figured that Tyrone would be gone forever from his house and his wife by the time that the second half began.

Unfortunately for Sandy, however, Tyrone was also very aware of the restrictions of time, and at the very moment that Sandy watched the big Longines-Wittnauer hands reach twelve together, Tyrone finished dressing and came down the stairs at Sandy's house, headed directly for Cynthia. He was dressed smartly in the uniform of Sergeant Ernest Kimberly, although his Afro bulged out so that it made it difficult for his Army cap to stay on his head. Tyrone went straight for Cynthia, who was sitting on the sofa, and kissed her ear before she knew what hit her.

"Cyn," said Tyrone, "listen to me." So she turned around to afford him more attention, and he took that as an invitation to kiss her full on the lips, which, in fact, he did straightaway. "Come with me."

"To Cuba?"

"Yes."

"Oh, Ty, don't be foolish." He put his hand on hers and looked at her in such a way that Cynthia was convinced that Tyrone was not just whistling "Dixie," even though he really was not likely to whistle "Dixie" under any circumstances. "But

I really don't want to go to Cuba. I don't even want to go to Puerto Rico."

"But I need you," Tyrone pleaded. "It won't just be Cuba, Cyn. There's a whole world out there waiting for us. There's Albania, North Korea, Algeria, the People's Congo, China, Tanzania." He put his arm around her and looked deep into her eyes. Cynthia was delighted with this affirmation of her allure —it certainly had been long enough in coming—but of course she also was concerned that she was too overflowing with charms for her own good. She managed to get her hand on the back of Tyrone's head and kind of push it down into her shoulder. The move was designed to suggest that she was drawing him closer to her; actually, it was an old trick that served to immobilize Tyrone while Cynthia tried to marshal her arguments.

"I can just see it," Tyrone said, turning his head to get a little speaking room. "Our own little corner of a commune outside Pyongyang or Peking or Brazzaville, just you and me before a roaring fire—"

"A roaring fire in Brazzaville?"

Tyrone ignored this nick in the reverie. "—with our little Pekinese or Borzoi at our feet, sipping rice broth, talking about the people's conquests of the day."

"It is a tender scene, Ty."

"Then you mean . . ."

"No, it's the little boy, Ty," Cynthia said, at last remembering an excuse. "You understand, I can't leave Teddy."

"We'll take him with us. We'll make him the first official citizen of the Third World."

"No, I really couldn't do that. I've already got Teddy enrolled in a good kindergarten." Cynthia also had to let Tyrone's head free at this point, since the way it was working out, she was pushing it not into her shoulder but onto her breast, and that was not at all what she had in mind. So Tyrone was able to reach up and kiss her jawline, which he really fancied.

"I lay awake nights, thinking of you there in the next room," he said. "Your hair, your eyes, your lips, your bones—"

"My bones?"

"The blood of African princesses coursing through your veins, the distilled beauty of a whole lush continent written across your face, the flames of an entire people's passions—"

"No, no, not here," Cynthia gasped. "And not Albania either."

"We owe ourselves one moment, our time, our secret."

"No, Ty," Cynthia said, shifting away from him and even straightening herself up prissily. "There's absolutely nothing you can say. I'm sorry, but there's nothing in the world that could make me change my mind."

Tyrone cursed to himself and thought anxiously. There must be something he could say. Even the stanchest woman has an Achilles heel in the right place. At least, if he couldn't get Cynthia to the Third World, he could get her up to the second floor. And suddenly it came to him. He withdrew his arm and leaned back, away from her. "Listen," he said dispassionately. "I don't come to you as a man, Cyn. Don't think of me as a man. Think of me only as your pro football."

Tyrone could see her perk up right away. Actually, the pages of Rosalie's last chapter, "Autumn Adultery: Alternative or Right?" were flipping before her mind's eye. "You see," Tyrone went on, "if Sandy can platoon his love for a whole season, then you can platoon yours for a mere afternoon."

"Wait a minute, Ty," Cynthia said, really coming to life. "An afternoon? I thought I had to do a whole tour in North Korea."

"I checked off when I saw the defenses," he explained.

Cynthia nodded and began to grin, finally expanding into a whole wicked smile, as she scanned Tyrone up and down, as if he were nothing less than a high draft choice. Then her eyes glittered. "I'll make a pass at you! Tackle me, Valentine!" Cynthia suddenly cried, and she reached up, threw both her arms about Tyrone's neck, and kissed him madly, as he systematically caressed her every bone.

A bit earlier, as Tyrone had started dressing up as Sergeant Ernest Kimberly, Ginger Toogood stood before her mirror at the Sheraton-Belvedere Hotel putting her clothes on too. She was only in a slip, but was carefully pinning her hair up on top of her head. She was definitely up to something: her hair was suddenly jet-black. When she finished piling it up, she picked up a nurse's little butterfly cap and pinned it into it. Then Ginger reached under the bed and drew out a large box. It contained a Red Cross uniform and white shoes, and she took them out and put them on too, stopping to admire herself in the mirror.

That done, she took the blond wig, the pair of hornrimmed glasses, and a large pair of barber's scissors that she had just purchased, and put them all into a little medical satchel, along with a couple of the bags that hotels provide to dispose of sanitary napkins in. Then Ginger locked her door from the inside, left through Toby's room, walked down two flights of stairs, and rang for the elevator on that floor.

The elevator operator did not recognize her; nor did the doorman when she asked for a cab. She told the driver, "Johns Hopkins Hospital, please," and with light Saturday traffic, the taxi made it in good time. Ginger paid, got out, and walked inside Hopkins to the hospital gift shop, where she bought a *Morning Sun* and some Cryst-O-Mint Life Savers. She went next to the ladies' room, into a toilet stall, where she took the wig and glasses from her satchel, wrapped them in sheets of the morning paper, stuffed these bundles into the sanitary-napkin bags, and dropped them both into the trash receptacle. In the lobby, at the huge statue of Jesus, Ginger cut the other way from where she had come in, and departed the hospital at the side clinic entrance. She flagged a Diamond cab there and said, "Pratt and Charles, please."

She got out at that corner, and as soon as the cab had sped away she walked up a half-block or so to the Hertz Rent A Car place on the other side of the street. Ginger smiled and said that she had a reservation. She laid her Maryland driver's license and a UniCharge card on the counter, took the full collision coverage, and agreed to return the car to this location.

"Is this street address one or two words?" the clerk said, studying her license.

"It's two words, hon. Capital M, O, double S; capital W, A, Y: 6205 Moss Way," Ginger Toogood said in a distinct Baltimore accent.

24

Meanwhile, Back to Live Action

The Colt offensive starting unit was introduced, one by one, but just before Unitas was waved out by himself for the final, greatest appreciation, the public-address announcer declared: "And not starting from scrimmage, but opening as a kick-returner: from West Point, Baltimore's own, Number 22, his rookie NFL appearance, Toby Geyser!" Toby had not antici-pated this individual introduction, and he forgot to put his helmet on, so that when he came up the steps through the first-base dugout and onto the field, funneled between two lines of the Colt marching band, his brown crew-cut gleamed in the high December sun, and the spectators in the stadium imag-ined that they could see a confident smile written across his handsome face.

The scene was painfully emotional. People stood and cried openly, cheering with such intensity that Unitas could not even hear the PA announce his name, so he at last just ambled out on his own. Only the playing of "The Star-Spangled Banner" brought some quiet to the stadium. "This is the way we'll start the recruiting movie," Unc Sam said to General Admire. The Colts had provided them with VIP seats near Section 10.

The roar began to build again after the anthem, even before the teams moved out on the field, simply because the referee signaled that the Colts had won the coin flip and would receive the opening kickoff. Toby buckled his helmet strap and burst from the team huddle to his position, just a step in front of the goal line. He was stationed on the right, alongside Alvin Haymond, who set up as the deep kick-return man on the other side of the field.

Don Chandler, the Green Bay kicker, teed the ball up. A teammate near him yelled, "Kick it right to the hero, Don," but Chandler couldn't hear a word in the din. He paced back and raised his arms, looking at the referee for a hand signal to begin. No one in the stadium moved, except way down at the other end of the field, where Reds Ritchie reached up to take off his Ricky, the Don't-Litter-Maryland's-Beautiful-Highways Raccoon head, because his tears had filled up the eyeholes.

Reds got the mask off just in time to see Chandler meet the ball. Whether intended or not, there was never any doubt that the ball was headed right for Toby. It was a magnificent long kick, too, holding high in the air as the Packers tore down under it. Toby backed up one step, then another, then still one more, so that he was almost four yards deep in the end zone when the ball came down into his arms. He was ready to put his knee down and ground the play with a touchback, giving the Colts a clean start on the 20-yard line, but he caught the ball perfectly and just as his body happened to rock forward naturally off his back heel. In that instant, even before he knew that he had made the decision, Toby's old instincts took him out of the end zone and straight up the middle of the field.

A Packer named Doug Hart hit him first, at the 12-yard line. Hart got knocked off balance at the last moment by a block from Preston Pearson, though, and all he did was throw Toby off stride, so that he shifted slightly to the left without even meaning to. When he did, he found himself in an opening and sprinted past two Packers who were cutting too fast the other way. Toby even got momentarily clear when Jim Welch took a third Packer clean off his feet right in front of the head lines-man. It was no clip. Another Packer, whom the films showed to be big Gale Gillingham, shook off a block but just missed forc-ing Toby out of bounds, and he was able to cut straight up the sideline. Suddenly he was free and racing past his own 35.

Chandler, the kicker, was the only Packer directly in his path, but Toby slowed down enough to let a teammate—it turned out to be Alex Hawkins—catch up, and he got Toby past Chandler with a shoulder block that let him cut back inside. There were still two Packers coming at him on an angle from way across the field, but Toby saw them out of the corner of his eye and churned up speed: past the 40, the 30, the 20.

At the 8-yard line, the green shirt closest to him had his best angle and lunged at him. Toby tried to yank his feet away in a drum-major's strut. The defender did succeed in getting a hand on his shoe, though, and Toby stumbled. He managed two steps upright, and then, as his balance went, he reached down with his free hand and, using it like a vaulter's pole, he pushed down on the ground and threw himself up and into the end zone. It was incredible. He made the touchdown by a foot, the longest kickoff return in Baltimore history. The official's hands shot into the air, and Ricky, the Don't-Litter-Maryland's-Beautiful-High-ways Raccoon, descended on Toby. Reds grabbed him and kissed him and pounded him and jumped up and down with him.

"That fucking coyote is going to ruin the picture," Unc Sam said. Everybody else in the stands was hugging and kissing. The game was only ten seconds along, but already kids were trying to get down onto the field. In Sandy's seats in Section 10 there was not a dry eye, and Mickey Shadducks, of Mickey Shadducks Olds, began to sing "The Caissons." "Up yours, Cheryl," he added as an afterthought.

The two teams, however, only drifted into a back-and-forth defensive game for the balance of the first quarter. The Packers couldn't even move when they recovered a Colt fumble early in the second period, and had to settle for a 36-yard field goal from Chandler. He kept the ensuing kickoff well away from Toby this time, but when Toby trotted off the field, the coach came over to him. "If we make a first down," he said, "you go in for Orr for a series." Promptly Lenny Moore made 5 yards off left tackle, and Unitas hit his tight end, John Mackey, for 7 more and the first down. Toby ran into the game.

All of Memorial Stadium rose to its collective feet.

Unitas acknowledged Toby in the huddle. "Look out, I'm working a lot of fast counts today," he said, and Toby nodded. Unitas called a pass pattern that had Raymond Berry, the split end, as the primary receiver. Toby flanked the other side from Berry, and, just as the coach had anticipated, the Packers put double coverage on him.

Unitas held up his hands to quiet the crowd and took the ball right after, on "hup." Toby ran out five steps, feinted and turned in, just in time to see Unitas fake pumping the ball his way, then whirl and drill it to Berry, who jumped to snare it, dragging his feet to stay in bounds. The play made 8 yards, to the Colt 36, and on second down, with Toby split wide as a decoy again, Unitas sent his fullback, Jerry Hill, plowing up the middle. The yardsticks were brought in to show that Hill had missed making a first down by 6 inches.

Unitas looked at Toby in the huddle, then glanced around at the others, then back at Toby. Then, without any discussion, he called the play: "Double wing. Right split. Sixty-eight. Flanker angle in. On hup. Ready, break." Toby stood momentarily stunned. Unitas was giving up a sure first down to gamble on a long pass.

Toby moved out to his flank. Set. "Hup." He took the same few steps as he had before, faked outside, and then dashed away downfield, slicing right over the middle. There was only one Packer defender on him this time, because Green Bay was stacked up for a line plunge, and Toby already had a step on his man when he saw the ball arching his way. Unitas had thrown it perfectly, and it dropped over his shoulder right into his arms just as he crossed the Packer 40. The defender, surprised, and now embarrassed too, gambled and leaped to bat the ball away, but he missed completely and fell to the ground. There was no other Packer within 15 yards of Toby when he sauntered into the end zone and into the mad embrace of Ricky, the Don't-Litter-Maryland's-Beautiful-Highways Raccoon.

The place went up for the proverbial grabs.

Toby had touched the ball twice, gained 166 yards, and made two touchdowns for Baltimore. Rosalie heard it on the radio on the way to the airport. "This is a storybook," the announcer said. "If Hollywood wrote this script, nobody would believe it." Tyrone Dancer, riding in a rented car with his contact to the same destination, heard it all too. "My man," he said with enthusiasm.

The Packers came back with their first long march of the half, however, and after Bart Starr passed to Boyd Dowler for another first down, Green Bay had the ball on the Colt 12-yard line, and there were still three minutes left in the half. On the very next play, though, Billy Ray Smith reached through and jarred the ball loose on a handoff, and Don Shinnick recovered for Baltimore. On the Colt sidelines, the coach grabbed Moore by the arm. "Sit this series out, Lenny," he said. "Let Johnny just run out the clock." Then he pointed to Toby and told him to go in for Moore at running back.

In the stands, as soon as Toby came back onto the field, it was Katy-bar-the-door. For example, in Section 10, Professor T.J. Trombley of the Johns Hopkins University scholarship board wet his pants.

Unitas wasn't for taking the easy way out, though. He crossed up the coach and everyone else by passing on first down. It went to Berry for a short gain. Toby, set behind the line as a running back with Hill, swung out as a safety valve on the play, and again on second down, when Unitas tried to reach Mackey over the middle. Dave Robinson batted that pass away, however, and the Colts were left with third and six on their own 15. The Packers, in their defensive huddle, set to watch for the pass to Berry again, or possibly a wild long bomb to Jimmy Orr.

Unitas had other ideas. "You know the thirty-specials, Geyser?" he asked in the huddle.

"Yeah," Toby said.

"Okay, then. Double wing. Left split. Thirty-five special. On one. Ready, break." It was an off-tackle play, and for the third time in the game Toby felt the ball at his ribs. As he took the handoff, just synchronized, he could see his big left tackle, Jim Parker, step back and in, hooking the Green Bay defensive end inside. Jerry Hill, leading interference, cleared out the linebacker, and the corner back, playing Berry for a pass, was caught leaning the other way. Toby dashed into an outside patch of freedom, and suddenly Mackey loomed up from nowhere and blocked the Packer safety right off his feet. Nobody laid a hand on Toby till he got to Ricky, the Don't-Litter-Maryland's-Beautiful-Highway's Raccoon, 85 yards away in the end zone. It was the first time Toby had ever run the ball from scrimmage, and it was easily the longest such running play in the history of the Colts' franchise.

Pandemonium reigned.

The fans poured out onto the field, heading in a phalanx toward Toby. Truly frightened, he huddled in Reds' soft arms, cowering from the approaching mob, but even then there is no telling what might have happened to him had not a uniformed guard suddenly come to the rescue. Shaking a menacing nightstick, he at least succeeded in keeping the happy mob at bay until some regular police showed up to drive it away. Reds and the guard, flanking Toby on either side, ferried him across the field to the relative safety of the Colts' bench, where he got another joyous reception from his teammates. The guard had to stay on to shoo photographers and more intrepid unofficial intruders away.

"Hey, thanks," Toby said. He really was grateful.

The guard merely replied with a knowing wink, however, and flipped out his badge—only it wasn't a badge on one side. On that side it was covered with green, and there was only one word on it, printed in red block letters. The word, of course, was: OVERLORD. "Don't you worry," the guard whispered out of the side of his mouth. "I'm watching your ass."

"Hey, you guys are everywhere," Toby said, standing up to get ready to run off to the locker room when the half ended.

"Don't be seen talking to me," the guard said, dragging his nightstick across his mouth so that no one could tell he was talking either. He was a mousy little fellow with a scraggly mustache he had just grown for this job, and some Clearasil dabbed in a couple of places. "You want to blow my cover?"

"Take it easy," Toby said. "How many agents you got working this case, anyhow?"

"Not so loud, for Chrissake. Don't say agent so loud. I'll see you after the game."

Now Toby was getting a little irked. Nobody had told him he had to go sneaking around hiding tape recorders, and nobody had told him there were going to be more DANG and DONG agents creeping up on him than Green Bay Packers. Besides, he liked it better working more cozily with Ginger. "Well, how many of you clowns, anyway?"

"Just me, that's all," the mousy little fellow said anxiously under his breath. "Keep it down, willya?"

Toby stopped dead in his tracks. "Just you? You mean that?"

"Look, I'm a senior agent, for Chrissake. I'm no undercover journeyman. I'm an S-8, chief grade."

"You mean there's no good-looking, stacked blonde working for you as an agent?"

The little guy chuckled. "Major, hey, you've been seeing too many spy movies."

Toby clapped himself on the head. "What a revoltin' development this is," he cried, and suddenly, worse, he could imagine exactly what had really been in that briefcase that Ginger had gotten him to hide at the Fifth Regiment Armory. He ran away so fast that he almost bowled over Ricky, the Don't-Litter-Maryland's-Beautiful-Highways Raccoon, who was just jogging off to get ready for his half-time ride in Santa Claus's sleigh.

25

Safety Blitz

The teams were coming out on the field for the start of the second half when the Colt general manager reached General Admire at his seat. Unc Sam was away getting a hot dog. "General," the man said in a desperate whisper, "I must be direct. Do you know where Major Geyser is?"

Admire rolled his licorice around. "How should I know? He's on T Dy. with the Colts."

"Sir, I hate to tell you this, but we can't find him."

"Whatdya mean? You can't miss him. He's Number 22."

"No, I mean he's disappeared," the general manager said, lowering his voice even more to make sure no one else heard. "Nobody has seen him since the Colts came off the field at half time. At first we thought he was in a toilet or something, but he's nowhere. He couldn't have gotten away from the stadium —his clothes are all still here—and we can't find him anywhere in it. It's like he's vanished into thin air."

Admire slapped his fist into his hand and said, "Kidnaped."

"You mean by Green Bay?"

"Of course not, you ninny. This involves the security of the whole nation," Admire said, rising from his seat. "Not a word of this to anyone. Not the TV, not the newspapers, not the public-address, not even the coach. Savvy?"

"Yes sir," the general manager shouted, so charged up that he saluted. Then, getting in step with Admire, he escorted the general to a private phone in his own office.

Admire locked himself in alone and rang up Colonel Beardsley at DANG headquarters. He didn't mince any words. "Beardsley, General Admire. Are you familiar with surgery? You are? Good, because it's nut-cuttin' time. Savvy?" He told the colonel to crank up all the machinery that would put DANG on alert, because Toby Geyser had been kidnaped, surely by Tyrone Dancer and his cohorts.

"The way I see it, Beardsley, Dancer and Tatler and that gang found out that Geyser was onto them, just as they were poised to use the National Guard to take over the country. No wonder they kidnaped him. Now, we got to strike back."

"Yes sir!" Beardsley yelled back into the phone.

"Far be it for me to be the first DANG commander to preside over the loss of the United States to a National Guard *coup*."

"Yes sir!" Beardsley cried again, and Admire slammed the phone down, rushed to the parking lot, and had his Pentagon chauffeur drive him lickety-split, sirens blaring, to Friendship Airport. That is where most of the DANG troops would be disembarking.

Unc Sam missed out on all this, because when he went to the press-room lounge to get a hot dog, he found there were crab cakes, so he stayed for two juicy ones, plus the extra one he took back to his seat. A Baltimore city patrolman caught up with him there, just as he was biting into his takeout crab cake.

"General," he said, "I'm afraid I have some really stinky news for you. There has been a huge explosion down at the Fifth Regiment Armory. It was like an H-Bomb hit."

Unc coughed at this report and spat out the crab cake, and the ketchup and the pickle relish, all over the officer. The pickle relish was really a bad break for the patrolman, but nobody back at the press lounge had had the nerve to tell Unc Sam that you didn't put pickle relish on a crab cake.

"That's that sonofabitch Tyrone Dancer, the militant," Unc bellowed, just as Lou Michaels' second-half kickoff arched into the sky. "He's the one blowing up National Guard armories. How many people were killed?"

"By the grace of God, no one, sir," the patrolman said, casually scraping the crab cake and its condiments off his uniform with his parking-violations book, so as not to call too much attention to what the general had done to him. "Even if no one was hurt, it still had to be the biggest explosion in Baltimore since Fort McHenry was bombarded—you know, 'The Star-Spangled Banner'—"

"You bet your ass I know 'The Star-Spangled Banner,' " Unc said and, polishing off the crab cake, he tore down to the parking lot. That was when he found his Pentagon car missing and realized how deep the plot to take over the National Guard really was. He commandeered a police car and, sirens blaring, he took off for the Armory, about three miles away.

Smoke was still pouring out of the huge old building when he drove up. It was a cavernous fortress, almost medieval in appearance, and once, long ago, a place of some glory. In the summer of 1912 the Democrats assembled there in the wet heat, finally nominating Woodrow Wilson after forty-six sweaty ballots. Now Unc assayed the old Armory from a safe distance.

"Don't worry, she's as sturdy as a rock," Sergeant Pat Mum of the Baltimore Police Department bomb squad reported to him. "Soon as this smoke clears out, you could hold a Guard meeting in there, or a dog show or whatnot."

Reassured, Unc came out of the car and joined Sergeant Murn, to inspect the scene closer up. "Just some kind of fancy smoke bomb, eh, Sergeant?"

Murn chuckled. "No sir! General, there was enough C-4 plastic in that charge to blow a small city off the map."

"Well, what the hell is this building doing still standing?" Unc demanded querulously.

Sergeant Murn said, "Can you stand a little smoke, sir?" And when Unc Sam assured him in no uncertain terms that he had swallowed more smoke than Sergeant Murn could ever hope to see, the officer led the way, and they ducked inside the Armory. Once they got past the vestibule into the yawning main hall, where the Guard drills, it was not too bad, because the ceilings were so high and the place was so vast and empty that the smoke had risen and thinned out down below. When they reached Colonel Tatler's office on the other side, however, much more smoke was still trapped in this small room, and both men had to keep their handkerchiefs to their faces.

Sergeant Murn steered Unc Sam across the room to the pile of Bingo Turf. It was scorched and frazzled and leaning somewhat to one side, and there was one pretty big hole in the middle, but all in all, it was still a pretty sturdy pile of Bingo Turf. Sergeant Murn patted it, even somewhat affectionately, and took his handkerchief away from his mouth to talk. "Whoever hid the bomb, put it right here in the middle of this stack, probably late last night or early this morning. Six–eight-hour timing device."

"What is this stuff?" Unc asked, holding his hand out tentatively.

"Go ahead, touch it, sir. It's okay. It's some kind of new artificial grass called Bingo Turf."

"Between you and I," Unc Sam said, "it feels like a piece of sandy pussy."

"Well, whatever, sir, from what we can tell, it's really something we're onto. You see, this Bingo Turf acted exactly like a whatchamacallit, an anecdote, to the bomb. There's nothing we ever saw like it before. You see how easy these fibers come off?"—and he pressed his hand down on a slice of Bingo Turf to illustrate the point. "Well, sir, somehow that property helps to contain the explosion. You get all your usual smoke and noise, but the bomb's real power is wasted dealing with the fibers. The way we figure it, the Bingo Turf somehow dissipates the explosive action, if you see what I mean."

Unc Sam said he certainly did and rubbed his hands tenderly over some more of the Bingo Turf. He had completely forgotten about keeping his handkerchief to his face by now; for that matter, he had completely forgotten about coughing. "Sergeant, this stuff could make explosive devices, as we know them, obsolete. I'll tell you what, being here, at this moment in history, is like standing out in the rain next to Ben Franklin, flying that half-assed kite of his when he invented electricity."

"Yes sir."

"So let's keep this on the QT."

"Yes sir."

"We don't want the Commies to get a line on Bingo Turf."

"No sir. I realize if this information fell into the wrong h—"

"Who makes Bingo Turf, anyway, Sergeant? Just as a point of interest."

Sergeant Murn took out his notepad and flipped a few pages. "I got it written down right here. It's a company out in Timonium called Cut 'N' Run, sir. Bingo Turf is a subsidiary of Cut 'N' Run."

"Is that so?" Unc Sam said. "Well, we better get a twenty-four-hour guard on this room and keep the door locked tighter'n a drum until we can get some of our A-one government boys to check this stuff out."

He and Sergeant Murn crossed back through the hall and went outside again into the fresh air. "The damage is certainly minimal," Unc assured the other officials there, "but there is still no doubt that this is an opening attack on the whole National Guard, bar none. We are teetering on the brink of a national emergency, and I want that building off limits to everyone. Now I've got to get my ass to a phone and head off this conspiracy from wiping out the whole Guard."

Sergeant Murn immediately volunteered his police radio, but, as Unc Sam pointed out, a police frequency would be one of the first things that militants would tap into. "No siree, we'll depend on good old Ma Bell herself," he said and, after borrowing a dime from Patrolman Ralph DiGrazio, he ran to a pay phone in the parking lot.

"Operator," he barked, "this is Major General Carlton Samuels, US Army, calling on the authority of the National Defense Security Act of 1954. You got that? . . . No, that's not a goddamn credit-card number. It's the National Defense Security Act of 1954—one, niner, five, four. Notify your superior."

He drummed his fingers impatiently, waiting for a supervisor to come on with his authorization. "Good," he said after a moment. "Now, I'll have two calls. The first one is to Alexandria, Virginia, area code 703, 751-9236."

The phone rang twice, and as soon as Unc heard his party answer at the other end he snuggled up close to the mouthpiece and whispered urgently, "Hello, Frieda, it's me, Unc. Now get a pencil and be quick about this, because I've got to get back to work and thwart a takeover of the whole National Guard. All right, you got it, Mother? Now, write this down: Cut 'N' Run. You got that? . . . Affirmative, Cut 'N' Run. It's the moniker of some little company up here in Maryland. Now,

Monday morning, first thing, I want you to get on the horn to Pottsy Caster down at Merrill Lynch, and I want you to tell him to buy every nickel of that sonofabitch he can lay his hands on. . . .

"That's right. I don't care how you get the money. Get us a second mortgage, borrow on the GI life, sell the cars, hock the Spanish Provincial, breed the dog, and for Chrissake, call up Parsons and tell them we got to temporarily stop payment on that tuition check I just mailed in for that hippie of ours. . . . Look, stop payment. In another couple months, he can buy his own college. You just get us Cut 'N' Run. Okay, over and out."

Unc Sam clicked the receiver and gave the operator the special number at DONG headquarters. Beardsley put General Admire on hold and came on the line. "Beardsley, this is General Samuels," Unc shouted into the phone. "This is urgent. Tyrone Dancer has started his move to destroy the National Guard. He just tried to blow up the main Armory here in Baltimore. The whole Guard is hanging by a thread, so we're putting DONG in effect. You hear me: I want it done no later than yesterday."

"But sir," Beardsley said, "General Admire called up just a little while ago, and he told me to activate DANG because Tyrone Dancer and Tatler are going to take over the Guard and pull a *coup* on the whole country. Can you see outside, sir?"

"Sure I can. I'm in a glass phone booth."

"Are you near downtown Baltimore?"

"Yes, Beardsley. What the hell is this, animal-vegetable-or-mineral?"

"If you just look up, sir, I think you'll see the first bunch of paratroopers from the 88th Airborne coming down now to work for DANG."

Beardsley was right. Unc could see the first specks falling out of the sky. "DANG, hell," he yelled. "This is a job for DONG."

"But sir, General Admire called first, and I've committed all the US troops to DANG."

"Well, goddamn it, you uncommit a few."

"But sir, I can't," Beardsley said. "We never had a contingency plan for DANG and DONG to get activated at the same time."

"Wait a minute, Beardsley," Unc Sam cooed suddenly, truly avuncular for a change, his voice soft and oily. "Now, I don't want you to blow a gasket. I want to help you. How would you like to get your little red ass on Easy Street forever?"

"Sir?"

"If you just get some of these troops shifted to my command at DONG, I'm going to give you a little stock tip that will set you up for life."

"Sir, I—uh—"

"Beardsley, would I kid you? I'm not giving you some nickel-dime high flyer like fucking bowling alleys or speedy fried chicken. I'm getting you in on the ground floor of a can't-miss proposition. This is like owning the patent on canned foods or Jackie Kennedy pictures."

"Gee, sir, I don't know," Beardsley said haltingly.

"This is going to be better than running PXs."

"*Yes sir*, I'll get you those troops," Beardsley cried.

"All right, now you're showing some horse sense. The name of the stock to buy"—and Unc leaned into the phone and whispered—"is Cut 'N' Run. Got it?"

"Cut 'N' Run? Yes sir."

"Okay, now I'm going out to the airport, and you fly me in some troops before Tyrone Dancer blows up any more armories." He slammed the receiver down and rushed over to the police car that would take him to Friendship Airport.

"You coming with me, Sergeant Murn?" Unc Sam asked. "I could use a man with your know-how in a crisis situation."

"Well, thank you, sir," Murn replied, "but a call just came through down at the stadium. I've got to get right down there and defuse a hot bomb. Somebody was caught trying to blow up Memorial Stadium."

"What a conspiracy," Unc Sam gasped. "That sonofabitch Tyrone Dancer is all over the place."

"No sir," Murn said. "I'm afraid there's no connection. It seems like the person trying to blow up the stadium was doing it to get back at pro football. She just keeps babbling about acting on behalf of all the women in America."

"Sounds like one of those far-out feminist nuts. Do they know her name?"

"No, General, she hasn't been identified yet. But it shouldn't be too hard. She's wearing a tailored Demolition Derby asbestos suit with an STP sticker on her thigh and the initials CS over her heart."

"No, don't know the lady," Unc said, and he climbed into the police cruiser. Hardly had the car cut down Howard Street, though, on the way to the airport expressway, when the roar began. It grew louder and louder, even with the sirens on full blast and the windows rolled up. It was a frightening, muffled thunder, like a hundred Niagaras pounding or a great barrage of distant guns. In fact, the first waves of DANG paratroopers, just now landing in Mount Vernon Square, were sure that it was a mighty fusillade aimed at them as they floated down defenselessly. Not till they were on the ground did they realize that it was only a chant coming from Memorial Stadium.

"We want Toby, we want Toby, we want Toby," went the angry cry, on and on. The crowd was growing ugly. It did not seem to even care about the MUST game itself any longer. There was no real reaction when Green Bay scored on a long march to make it 21–10. The people just kept screaming for Toby.

In Sandy's Section 10 seats, people had all but stopped even

watching the game. Instead, they were devoting themselves entirely to scanning the sidelines with their binoculars, hoping to
find Toby there, or peering into the baseball dugout, looking
for the first sign of his return to the field. Jerry was studying the
Colts' bench for, as he told Mickey Shadducks, "the umpteenth
time" when he did catch sight of something interesting, even
if it didn't have anything to do with where Toby was. It was
the lonely figure of Reds Ritchie standing on the sidelines way
down by the end zone, his collar up against his neck, his hands
thrust deep into the pockets of his parka.

Jerry was just about to stop chanting "We want Toby" and
inquire of Charlie Weaver why Reds would not still have on his
Ricky, the Don't-Litter-Maryland's-Beautiful-Highways Raccoon
outfit, but unfortunately he never got the chance, for it was just
at that moment that the elite DANG patrol showed up and
arrested him, Sandy, and Sergeant Topper, charging all three
with the attempted overthrow of the United States government.

26

Escape Routes

Toby flipped the cab driver a ten that Reds had given him and scampered into the airport. He started to take his raccoon head off to make it easier to run, but as soon as he entered the lobby he spotted General Admire, standing atop a large MARYLAND, AMERICA IN MINIATURE vacation display. Up there, the general seemed to command the whole lobby, barking orders to the troops that were already assembling around him, and to Colonel Beardsley, who was on the other end of a special direct line to DANG headquarters.

Regular United States Army troops assigned to DANG had already taken over National Guard armories in thirty-two states, the District of Columbia, and the Virgin Islands, and, just to be sure, had also assumed command of nearby Fort Meade and several Army recruiting centers as well. "Thirty-four," General Admire suddenly screamed as Toby snuck by him unobtrusively, holding up his little sign that said, "Hi! I'm Ricky, the Don't-Litter-Maryland's-Beautiful-Highways Raccoon!" so no one would think he was the enemy or anything. "You hear that, men?" Admire bellowed. "Thirty-four. We just secured Vermont and Iowa too. Let Tyrone Dancer put that in his pipe and smoke it."

Toby managed to get through the lobby encampment unmolested, and then broke into a run as soon as he turned down the corridor that led to the Pan American flights. In fact, he overtook and tore right past Tyrone and Ginger near the Allegheny counter, because he did not recognize them, especially from behind. Ginger, in her trim little Red Cross outfit, was pushing Tyrone along in a wheelchair. He was all spiffed up in his sergeant's uniform and was nearly unrecognizable anyway, because Ginger had cut off his Afro.

Sadly for Tyrone, it had occurred to Ginger while she was watching Toby shave that morning that Tyrone would have to be neatly shaven and his hair closely trimmed if he were to effect his military disguise. Consequently, she showed up much earlier at the Tatler household than had been agreed upon, because she would have to take the time to cut his hair there. To be precise, Ginger had knocked on the door just at the point when Tyrone had finally gotten down to Cynthia's beautiful bare bones. She sure shot a lot of holes in the game plan.

She had put Tyrone in such a rotten mood, as a matter of fact, that he really never got over the disappointment. Thereafter whenever he heard the word "Afro," it would remind him of how his Afro had cost him the one chance in a lifetime of making it with Cynthia, and it would drive him into a blue funk for hours on end. Tyrone, and all the people around him, always used the expression "natural" instead, and there is even an increasing body of thought which holds to the conclusion that the primary reason why the term "blacks" is preferred to "Afro-Americans" is directly traceable to this incident.

In any event, while Tyrone simmered in disgust in his wheelchair, still fretting about lost bliss, Toby dashed about looking for Ginger and him. He ran all the way down to the gate and then back to Pan Am's ticket counters, but he still could find no sign of them. It was getting on to just a few minutes before flight time when he popped into the men's room to check for Tyrone in there. It was empty, so Toby jumped next door to the ladies' room, although, of course, he made certain to leave his "Ricky" sign outside in the corridor. Unless you are really up on it, it is very hard to tell the sex of a raccoon right off. Ginger wasn't there, but Rosalie was. He had almost forgotten about her. "Come on, Rosie," Toby hollered at her, "help me find Dancer." He grabbed her by the hand, and they dashed outside, almost colliding with Tyrone's wheelchair as they ran out the door.

Toby took his head off. "My man," said Tyrone.

"Don't you my-man me."

"Hey, I got the negative, I got the picture," Tyrone said hurriedly, his little ears bristling with surprise at Toby's harsh tone.

"I don't care about them," Toby snarled.

"You don't?" asked Rosalie, hurt. Of course she still didn't know about Ginger Toogood at all, much less that she was a double agent and things of that nature.

Toby didn't bother to explain. Instead, he just turned on Ginger. "I only want to know one thing from you—and quick. When does that bomb go off?"

"Major, whatever bomb do you mean?"

"Don't get rough, Mr. Touchdown," Tyrone said softly but menacingly. "Remember, I'm carrying a gun to hijack the plane with."

Toby ignored him. "Now listen to me, Ginger Toogood," he said. "Don't be cute. I can take it that you fooled me, because somehow you worked your way in and fooled all DANG and DONG too, but I can't take it if you used me to kill a lot of

innocent people with that bomb. Now, come on, when does it
go off?"

Ginger smiled dumbly and put her hand down softly on his
paw. "Toby, that bomb has gone off—oh, forty, forty-five minutes ago."

He threw his raccoon head to the ground in anger. "You
bastards," he said.

"Hey, Toby," Tyrone said, and he reached up from his chair
and stroked Toby's fur compassionately. "Nobody was even
hurt."

"They weren't?"

"Of course not. Don't you see, we've discovered an antisep-
tic bombing. You just wait till the middle of a big pro football
game, and you can blow up anything without hurting anybody.
Everybody's away watching the game. And we're just playing
another game."

"I didn't kill anybody?"

"Now, would we do that to you, Toby?" Ginger asked.

"We only want to bring down the imperialistic, racist, mili-
taristic Establishment—the buildings, the trappings of deca-
dence and oppression," Tyrone explained. "Not the people; we
are the people."

Ginger shook her head sympathetically and resumed pushing Tyrone's wheelchair along to the gate. "Do you mean you
left your game and came all the way out here just for this?" she
asked him. Toby could only nod sheepishly in reply.

"Oh, you silly goose, you," she said.

Suddenly Tyrone came to life, slapping his hands together
and almost forgetting himself and rising right out of his wheelchair. "Wait a minute, everybody," he screamed. "We can still
turn this into a plus. You two come along with us."

"That's a neatsy idea, honey," Ginger cried, joining in.

"These things are always more fun when you've got another couple along."

"Gee," Toby said, brightening, but Rosalie tugged at his arm and shook her head.

"I really couldn't leave my kids," she said.

"And you know," Toby added, just trying to be polite, "I really don't think Cuba is me. Nothing political, you understand, Ty. It's just not the kinda place I would pick out."

"Well, it doesn't absolutely have to be Cuba," Ginger said. "We could always just go to a Swiss embassy. You hear such great things about them."

"Which one?" Rosalie asked.

"Oh, practically any one, I suppose. You know, just everybody who's been in a spot swears by them. If you don't want to get too far away from your kids, I don't see why we just don't drive down to Washington and take refuge in the Swiss embassy there."

"Well," Toby said. He wasn't real sure that you could take refuge in your own Swiss embassy.

"Look, it's certainly no trouble," Ginger went on brightly. "I haven't even turned the Hertz car in yet."

"No, thanks so much, Ginger, but I really think maybe I ought to get back to the game. They're probably wondering about me."

"Well, all right," Ginger said. "I forgot all about that."

They had almost reached the gate by now, and so Ginger stopped pushing Tyrone's chair and reached up and unpinned her little nurse's cap. The negative and the picture were clipped to the inside of it, and she took them off and handed them to Rosalie, who held the negative up to the light and, satisfied, grimaced and slipped it and the picture into her cleavage. Over the loudspeaker, the final call for Pan American flight 87 urged all passengers to get on board, and Tyrone pulled out the tickets and handed them to Ginger.

"You know something I just remembered, sweetheart?" he said, shaking his head at himself. "We forgot to make the phone call."

"Oh, you're right," Ginger said, and she slapped her forehead. "It never fails. You think you've gone over everything for a trip, and then there's always one thing you forget at the last moment—stop the mail or get someone to water the plants, or whatever."

"Well, we blew it," Tyrone said, watching the rest of the passengers winding down the ramp to get on board. "We just don't have time to get to a phone now." Ginger shrugged and went over to the counter to hand the tickets in.

"Listen, Ty," Rosalie suddenly said. "If it's just a phone call, I'm sure I could do it for you."

"Oh, that would be so nice of you."

"Who do I have to call?"

"Well, you really get quite a choice," Tyrone said. "Just when you get a chance, go into a pay booth and call up the police if you want, or a newspaper or television station, and tell 'em what revolutionary group you're with."

"Well, gee, I'm not with any group."

"Oh, yeah, you're not affiliated. Well, then, just tell them that you're a freelance working with Tyrone Dancer and that it was me who blew up the Fifth Regiment Armory, blah, blah, blah."

"You want them to know?"

"Of course," Tyrone explained. "There's certainly no sense blowing these things up if you're going to hide your light under a bushel."

"Well, okay, I can manage that."

"Gee, you're a real lifesaver, Rosalie. And you know, just ad lib a little, blah, blah, blah."

"Well, we're all set to go," Ginger said, coming back, "I ordered you a steak medium-rare and a very sturdy Beaujolais." Then she turned to Rosalie and winked broadly. "Hey now, Miz Start," Ginger said. "Dan't ferget to tell yur old man Jer that Chickie wan't be arrand hannlin' the phanes down Pine Brothers any more. Okay, hon?"

"Chickie—I knew there was someone you reminded me of," Rosalie said, snapping her fingers.

Ginger fished in her pocketbook and came up with some keys. "You take these, Toby," she said. "I hate to see them go to waste. There's a Hertz car—it's a blue Impala—out in the lot you can use to get back to town, and I've been in a little house in Glen Burnie that's got till the first of the year to run on the lease. I hate to see it go to waste. You might as well use it. It's just up from the Harundale Mall by the Royal Crabhouse: 6205 Moss Way."

"Gee, thanks," Toby said, taking the keys. Ginger reached up and gave him a little kiss on the cheek too, and then she grabbed hold of Tyrone's chair and began to roll him away through the gate and then down the ramp toward the plane. They both waved back, and Toby called out, *"Bon voyage."*

"A fun couple," Rosalie offered in valedictory, and she stood with Toby and looked out until the big jet shuddered down the runway and lifted off, gleaming in the sun. In counterpoint, across the way, they could also see the first waves of military planes landing with the Third Army and elements of the Eighth and Ninth Armored Brigades. The troops rushed toward the airport gates, zigzagging and keeping low, as if they were under heavy fire, and then they ran past Toby and Rosalie on the way to the lobby, in gas masks, with fixed bayonets.

"What's going on, anyway?" Toby asked a sergeant with a clipboard who was strolling along toward the coffee machine.

"Oh, it's a national emergency," the sergeant said. "Either the National Guard is pulling off a *coup* to take over the whole country, or somebody is taking over the National Guard and wiping it out. It's one or the other. There's a couple of generals in the lobby still arguing about these details."

27

Playing Them
One at a Time

The lobby had become even more chaotic, with troops packing it, most of them lounging on the floor, listening to the blurred hum of a thousand transistor radios. "So, for the first time this afternoon, Green Bay moves into the lead," Toby heard, as he and Rosalie picked their way through the soldiers. General Admire was still standing up on his MARYLAND, AMERICA IN MINIATURE display, but across the way Unc Sam had set up his DONG headquarters on an even more advantageous site, commandeering a large revolving presentation that was devoted to extolling the virtues of eating a lot of crabs.

Unc was perched, in fact, on a large plastic see-through crab cake that topped the exhibit, and he was gesticulating with a crab net, employing it rather like a saber in an effort to encourage the new troops to join his side. The National Guard armories had fallen to DANG and General Admire in three more states, but in six states, including California and the strategic whole Mississippi Delta area, DONG and Unc Sam had taken the upper hand.

In fact, so much activity was swirling around Unc on his crab cake that Toby decided to cut across the lobby the other way, toward General Admire, who was more accessible. "Sir," an aide cried, running past Toby and Rosalie as they neared Admire's command post, "we've taken Fort Holabird down in South Baltimore, and we got three battalions marching hard up Route 40 toward the Aberdeen Proving Grounds."

"Push on, push on," Admire cried. "And don't let that Unc Sam get any more men. Soon as we mop up this National Guard *coup*, we're going to go right after his ass." He screamed some more orders into the phone for Beardsley, just as Toby and Rosalie wormed their way up to the base of the display.

"How's it going, General?" Toby cried.

"Terrific, Geyser. The National Guard will never overthrow this country as long as I'm in the driver's seat. Savvy?"

"You bet I do, sir."

The general bit off some licorice. "We got the rat bastards who personally cooked up this *coup*, too. You familiar with anatomy, Geyser?"

"A little, yes, sir."

"Well, let me assure you: cut off the head and the body dies. Savvy? We haven't laid our hands on that Tyrone Dancer yet, but we just went out to the stadium and we arrested the brains behind this insurrection—that nigger Tatler and his two side-kicks too."

Toby could feel Rosalie's hand slide nervously down his arm until she could clasp his paw. "Who's that, General? Who's the sidekicks?"

"What's the other instigators' names?" Admire bellowed into a field telephone. "Yeah, Roger, the other guys with those fifty-yard-line seats." He put the receiver back down and turned to Toby. "The other plotters are a full-time sergeant E-6 named Topper and an NG speedy-four named Start." Rosalie swooned into Toby's arms. "We're trying to get confessions out of those would-be Benedict Arnolds right now."

Toby propped Rosalie up at his side and fanned her face a little. "They're safe, the instigators, aren't they, sir?"

"Don't you worry," Admire said. "We want them alive to testify at their own trial. We got 'em locked up under a heavy guard in a service-station men's room up by the stadium. Of course they're still denying everything, all three of them."

"Traitors always do," said Toby.

"They won't admit the first thing. They won't admit they even know of the plot to turn the National Guard against the US," the general went on. "They won't even admit that they kidnaped you— Wait just a cotton-pickin' minute." General Admire suddenly looked as if he had chanced across a real bad smell. "Hey, if you're kidnaped, why aren't you already killed or being held for ransom?"

"But I'm not, sir."

"Hell, you got to be. That's why DANG was called out in the first place. Tyrone Dancer and the other instigators kidnaped you when they learned that you knew they were going to turn the National Guard against the US. Now, what the hell are you doing running around in this woodchuck get-up?"

"It's a raccoon."

"I don't care if it's a porcupine or boa constrictor. That's a weak excuse when you're supposed to be kidnaped."

"I'm afraid you just got the wrong poop, sir."

"Well, isn't that a fine how-do-you-do?" Admire said in some disgust. He began pacing back and forth on the vacation display, pausing to lean on the mountainous part of the map, up by Cumberland. "This puts everything in a different light," he finally said, reaching for his special phone. "Beardsley, Beardsley, would you believe we better hold our horses? It looks like maybe we won't need those NATO troops from Scotland and Belgium after all."

"I'm sorry, sir," Beardsley reported from the other end, "we were just now notified that they've passed the point of no return over the Atlantic."

"The bagpipe band and all?"

"Yes sir, the whole bag of cheese."

"Holy shit. Listen, Beardsley, to let the cat all the way out of the bag, I don't even know if there's still a need for DANG holding Fort Meade. The thing of it is, Geyser isn't kidnaped at all. Savvy? He's standing here right now, dressed up in some monkey suit like a beaver."

Toby said, "Tell the colonel that Tyrone Dancer has skipped the country too."

"That's impossible," Admire said. "Unc just told me that Dancer bombed the Armory downtown this morning."

"Well, he did," Toby explained. "He did that, and then he hijacked a plane to Cuba."

"Would you believe that's the first I heard of that?"

"Well, it's imminent," Toby said.

"I got to talk to Unc and get this whole thing ironed out," Admire said forlornly. "Nothing's working out. Whether the National Guard is trying to take over the United States or whether it is someone trying to rub out the Guard, we can't find anybody in the National Guard. They're all over Robin Hood's barn watching the goddamn football games. It's hard to believe, isn't it?"

"Yes sir, it certainly is."

"Well, to tell you the truth, Geyser, it isn't so hard to believe. Are you familiar with the Viet Cong? Well, the National Guard is beginning to remind me of them. You can't lay your hands on either one of them. They're both slippery and elusive. If any of these Commies ever try to pull a fast one and come in here and take over this country when everybody is watching pro football, like during the Super Bowl, they're going to get another think coming.

"Sure, they could sneak right past the DEW line, sure they could waltz right into our nation's capital, but then they'd have to contend with the National Guard."

"I never thought of it that way before," Toby admitted.

"Neither had I, Major. But now I can see, during the football season, the National Guard is the most facile home defense we've had since the Minute Men. They're everywhere and nowhere. I'd rather fight the Cong than the Guard any day. If the Russkies or Chinee or any of that crowd ever tried to take over America, they'd be bogged down here for years, trying to employ conventional warfare against the National Guard. They'd never see the light at the end of the tunnel."

"That's really reassuring," Toby said.

"Well, now, remember, it's just that way during the pro football season. The rest of the time the Guard isn't watching the games, and they're hanging around the armories acting just like the National Guard. Then, of course, they're sitting ducks."

"Yes sir."

"What we got to do now, Geyser, to keep this country safe, we got to make it a federal law for the pro football season to go on twelve months a year."

"Gee, I don't think the women would go for that, sir," Toby suggested.

"Well, they'll just have to learn to like it, just like they're learning to like Vietnam. Savvy?"

"Yes sir," Toby said, saluting. "I'm sorry, sir, we've got to take off now. We got to make a phone call."

"Well, okay," General Admire replied, returning the salute.

"Naturally, I'm sorry you're not kidnaped, but me and Unc can parley and straighten this all out. Don't you worry."

Toby took a firm hold on Rosalie's hand and steered her around and between the soldiers. They covered the whole lobby wall-to-wall by now and were even spilling down into the corridors. The transistor hum was rising too. "Once again, the Colts have to give up the football," Toby heard the announcer say while he dragged Rosalie through the leering uniform masses over to a phone booth off in the corner. She put in a dime and dialed central police headquarters.

"Hello," Rosalie said, "and listen to me close, you fat pig, because I'm only going to say this one time. You dig? I'm calling for my man, Tyrone Dancer, and it was us who just blew the Fifth Regiment Armory to kingdom come. And that's just a start, too. Until the people in Baltimore get their rights, we're going to blow up a building a day. You read me, piggy?"

"You're doing real good," Toby whispered to her. "You sound real authentic. I hope they're making a tape of this so we can hear it on the news."

Rosalie smiled modestly and went on. "And one more thing, rat daddy. When you get that rubble that was the Fifth Regiment Armory cleaned up, you tell all the other white mothers in your racist establishment that Tyrone Dancer says they better not put another murder hotel up on that spot. We want a people's— Excuse me?"

Rosalie suddenly stopped to listen, and Toby saw a quizzical expression come over her face. "Oh no, I wasn't aware of that," she said. "No, I didn't know." And then: "Is that so? . . . I see. . . . Oh no, no need to worry about that. That's not in the works. . . . Right, promise. . . . Okay, 'by for now." She hung up the phone softly.

"What's the matter, Rosie?"

"Well, first of all, it didn't blow up."

"The Fifth Regiment Armory didn't?" Toby asked.

"Not at all." The phone rang, and it was the operator requiring another five cents in toll charges. Luckily, Rosalie had another nickel in her purse, and she dropped it in the slot. "No, the nice officer I spoke to said there was just a whole lot of smoke and stuff."

"That's funny. You wouldn't think Tyrone and Ginger would miscalculate so," Toby said.

"But the really weird part is that then the cop on the phone just started talking about Bingo Turf. That's all he wanted to talk about."

"Well, that's where I put the bomb—right in the stack of Bingo Turf that Sandy and Jerry keep piled up there in the office."

"There's something about Bingo Turf, that's for sure," Rosalie said. "The only thing the officer was concerned about was whether or not we were going to blow up the New York Stock Exchange before he could buy Cut 'N' Run on Monday morning. He didn't seem to care about bombing the Armory at all, except one time he did tell me to thank Tyrone Dancer for introducing him to Cut 'N' Run."

"What do you suppose that means?"

"I haven't got the foggiest," Rosalie said, scratching her head. "All I know is that no matter what happens these days, Cut 'N' Run just goes up some more."

"Yeah," Toby said. "Hey, let's get out of here, Rosie."

"Where do you want to go?"

"I don't know. Do you want to get something to eat—a hamburger or something?"

"No, Toby, I'm really not hungry."

"Well, neither am I, really. Listen," he said suavely and nonchalantly, as if the thought had just occurred to him. "If Jerry's locked up in a men's room somewhere under arrest for treason, there's a real good chance he won't be home for a while. I mean, I don't want to be opportunistic or anything, but you know, Rosie, Ginger Toogood gave me the keys to her house, and it's just over in Glen Burnie."

Rosalie looked up at him and ran her tongue over her teeth. "Okay," she said. "We're still owed one."

"That's the spirit," Toby said, and he handed her the house key. "You go on ahead. I got to find Ginger's car in the lot. The house is up from the Harundale Mall by the Royal Crabhouse."

It took Toby some time to find Ginger's car, but that didn't upset him, because he knew that that just gave Rosalie more time to get herself properly ensconced in Ginger's bed, which she did. By the time he turned off at the Royal Crabhouse and came cruising down Moss Way, checking the numbers for the right house, Rosalie had already pulled down all the shades in the bedroom, tidied up the place, and propped herself up in bed. She sat there, combing her hair in the dim light, and practiced looking tawny.

Toby spotted the house—a one-story shingled bungalow like all the others on the block—but just to be discreet he drove a few more houses down the street before pulling over to park. He was just getting out of the car when Jerry came down the street behind him and pulled his Mustang right into the space in front of 6205. If Jerry hadn't been so worked up, he would have noticed that it was his wife's station wagon in the driveway.

Toby saw Jerry striding up the walk and scurried behind a mailbox. That was when several people on the block called the police, and even though Toby wasn't wearing his raccoon head any longer, two called the ASPCA. Toby waited there, crouched behind the mailbox, until he saw Jerry step inside the house. Then he dashed back to the car, jumped in it, and gunned away, whistling *La Traviata* to give himself strength.

As soon as she heard the door open, Rosalie called out, "I'm in here. What kept you?"

Jerry shut the door and started walking toward the bedroom. "Would you believe," he said, "I was being held for treason. They just now let me go."

The instant she heard him, even before she saw him in the doorway, Rosalie knew who it was. She didn't know what to say, so she said, "Hi, Jerry."

"Rosalie," said Jerry. "Uh, how are you?" He didn't know what to say either.

"Just fine, thanks. How did the game go?"

"Oh, not so good. After Toby disappeared, the Colts fell all apart and the Packers won." He took a couple of tentative steps into the bedroom.

"So now the season's finally over. Right?"

"Yes, it's all over for the Colts."

"Well, if the season's over, why don't you come over here with me, sweetheart?"

"Oh sure, yeah," he said, and he came over and stood by the side of her bed. Rosalie reached out and touched him, and when she did, the sheet fell away to her waist. He smiled shyly and took off his coat and his shirt, and even before he could undo his belt, Rosalie reached up, put her arms around his neck, and sort of hung on him, her head on his chest. He sat down on the bed next to her and held her in his arms.

Rosalie looked up into his eyes. "I'm sorry, Jerry," she said. "Please don't be upset. This doesn't have to happen ever again."

"You're telling me, Baby Cakes," he said. "If we can just get a couple of big strong linemen in the draft who have real good pursuit, there's no reason why we can't beat the Packers next year and go all the way."

Where Are They Now?

1973 Thumbnail Sketches of All the Main Characters *

ROSALIE START had her third child, a second daughter, Hilary, early in September of 1968. In May of that year she had met Paul Newman at a McCarthy for President rally in New York, but their conversation was brief and uneventful. Rosalie has felt that the fact that she was five months pregnant at the time helped account for his apparent indifference. Now the president of the Metropolitan Baltimore Coordinated Women's Liberation League, Rosalie favors an IUD and wears granny glasses for driving.

JERRY START was elected a full partner of Pine Brothers and Moore on January 4, 1969. Following Kempton Moore's untimely death when he was evidently mistaken for a low-flying canvasback duck by a well-armed Mrs. Moore, the firm was officially renamed Pine Brothers and Start on January 1, 1971. Jerry had also been elected to the board of directors of Cut 'N' Run by the time that company was

* In order of appearance.

sold to ITT early in 1969. The Start family received $29,-472,890 in ITT stock in that transaction. The Starts sold their house in Ruxton shortly thereafter and moved to a 360-acre estate in the fashionable Green Spring Valley, north of Baltimore, where Jerry has invested heavily in thoroughbred horses. He and Rosalie also own resort houses in Hobe Sound, Florida, and Portugal, and a cooperative duplex apartment on Park Avenue in New York City. Jerry was the head of a three-man syndicate which offered $17.4 million in May 1972 to buy the Baltimore Colts from the then owner, Carroll Rosenbloom, who had threatened to move the team to Tampa.

TOBY GEYSER abruptly resigned his commission in February 1968 and made sporadic, if impressive, appearances for the balance of the year on behalf of the presidential candidacy of Dick Gregory. Toby dropped from sight shortly thereafter, growing a large beard to help in his pursuit of anonymity, only to emerge as "the other man" in the spectacular divorce trial of movie actress Toni Winston and producer Karl Anders. In November 1970, in Seaford, Delaware, Toby married seventeen-year-old Karen Walker Tremont, the famous young "Green Heiress." Karen is the daughter of the late T.L. Tremont, who made a fortune when he invented, patented, and then sold to the government the shade of green that appears on every interstate road sign in the United States. The couple, who reside in Rancho Santa Fe, near San Diego, are presently expecting their first child. Toby has invested heavily in group-therapy parlors throughout the Southwest.

GENERAL ADAM ADMIRE retired from the service in 1969 to join Mighty, Inc., a defense firm, after concluding his

Army career with command of the America division in Vietnam. The general lives in Alexandria, Virginia, in a spacious mobile home.

GENERAL CARLTON ("UNC SAM") SAMUELS left the Army early in 1968, only weeks after placing his life savings in Cut 'N' Run stock and seeing his investment multiplied twenty-seven times. Presently the general is writing his memoirs, *No Bullet With My Name on It*, at his palatial retirement home in Wrightsville, New Jersey.

COLONEL ROGER BEARDSLEY also separated from a career in the service a few weeks after so felicitously investing in Cut 'N' Run. Since a recent marriage ended in divorce, with heavy alimony payments, the forty-two-year-old multimillionaire occupies his time by doing gardening commentaries for a local radio station near his home in Paradise Valley, Arizona.

SANDY TATLER left Pine Brothers and Start in the spring of 1971 to assume the presidency of Why Not? Inc., a firm that specializes in black investment in suburban areas. A rift among black political leaders caused Sandy to sit out the 1971 Baltimore mayoralty campaign, but all black support, and much white as well, has coalesced behind him, and he is expected to be an across-the-board reform candidate for mayor in 1975—if he does not decide to hold out for another year and bid for the senate seat in 1976 that is presently occupied by Republican Glenn Beall, Jr. Sandy resigned all association with the National Guard following the summer camp of 1968, when his commitment was up.

CYNTHIA TATLER had her second son, Robert Nyerere, in

September 1968 at the Greater Baltimore Medical Center. The child was born exactly three hours (although a calendar day) later than Hilary Start. Cynthia, who does needlepoint and does not wear bras, is expected to be accepted in the Junior League. Her older son, Theodore, has entered the Child Training Class at Calvert School, and the Tatlers were the first black family to settle in fashionable Guilford, moving to a Greenway address near the Sherwood Gardens early in 1970. Cynthia has become active in her community Zero Population Growth council and can often be seen on local educational TV channels in that capacity.

Young Skippy Benton sold all his holdings in Cut 'N' Run and placed his entire fortune in municipal bonds before leaving on a leisurely round-the-world trip in January 1969. Going west, he has reached Holiday Inn No. 6, in the Greater Pittsburgh area, where he is presently shacked up with a onetime nun named Carla Poole.

Reds Ritchie married the former Gracia McAdams of Baltimore on St. Valentine's Day, 1971, at the Church of the Redeemer. Reds has been honored three years running for producing life-insurance sales of better than $1,000,000, and for this achievement his picture once appeared in a full-page advertisement in *Look* magazine. The Ritchies have moved to the planned city of Columbia, Maryland, where Reds is head of the Residents' Interracial Council. The Ritchies' first child, a son, Harold Howard IV, was born in November 1972.

Tyrone Dancer re-entered the United States, via Mexico, with a false passport in October 1969. He is still living under an assumed name, probably somewhere in the San Francisco area, although friends who have spoken to him lately report that he may be anxious to travel to China and resettle there. Tyrone is able to live comfortably because the sale of a hundred shares of Cut 'N' Run brought him close to $1,000,000. In April of 1972 he unexpectedly appeared one night at Toby Geyser's home in Rancho Santa Fe and presented him with a bottle of champagne and a box of the finest Cuban cigars. After a brief conversation, Tyrone then left quickly in a dune buggy, and Toby has not heard from him since.

GINGER TOOGOOD was able to escape from Cuba, somehow managing to pass herself off as the wife of a British journalist named Evans, only two days before it was discovered that she was a triple agent whose true identity and allegiance were known to only three men in the CIA. She returned to the United States in May 1968 and later, under the name of Daisy Champion, was eventually revealed as the so-called "Lady in the Tiara" who appeared so regularly in diplomatic circles in Peking in the weeks leading up to Henry Kissinger's initial secret meeting there with Chou En-lai. Married briefly to Colonel (ret.) Roger Beardsley of Paradise Valley, Arizona, Ginger completely stumped the panel of *What's My Line* on the show of August 18, 1972. Arlene Francis came closest, guessing that Ginger was a professional bowler.